100

THINGS TO DO IN
SHREVEPORT-BOSSIER
LOUISIANA
BEFORE YOU
DIE

Shreveport Common

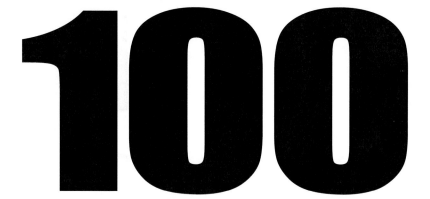

100

THINGS TO DO IN
SHREVEPORT-BOSSIER
LOUISIANA
BEFORE YOU
DIE

MONICA DOLLAR CHAMPAGNE

REEDY PRESS

Library of Congress Control Number: 2023951760

ISBN: 9781681065205

Design by Jill Halpin

All images were provided by the author unless otherwise noted.

Printed in the United States of America
24 25 26 27 28   5 4 3 2 1

We (the publisher and the author) have done our best to provide the most accurate information available when this book was completed. However, we make no warranty, guarantee, or promise about the accuracy, completeness, or currency of the information provided, and we expressly disclaim all warranties, express or implied. Please note that attractions, company names, addresses, websites, and phone numbers are subject to change or closure, and this is outside of our control. We are not responsible for any loss, damage, injury, or inconvenience that may occur due to the use of this book. When exploring new destinations, please do your homework before you go. You are responsible for your own safety and health when using this book.

DEDICATION

To my husband, Stephen, and children, Clara and Conley, who
are always on board for the next adventure.

To my parents, Lauren and Larry, for the carefree, laid-back
Louisiana upbringing.

To the eclectic Shreveport-Bossier community who
supported the writing of this book by welcoming me
into their establishments.

CONTENTS

• •

Music and Entertainment

• •

Sports and Recreation

● ●

• •

Culture and History

• •

Shopping and Fashion

• •

PREFACE

Born and raised in Shreveport, Louisiana, I come from a family of six generations that called Shreveport home. Having lived there for over 30 years, its friendly people, unique charm, history, and delicious food have always held a special place in my heart. Most recently, I have been highlighting United States travel itineraries and things to do for road-tripping families through my blog champagneondeck.com. I decided that it was finally time to share with my readers the aspects of my hometown, Shreveport, that make it such a special and unique place.

These days, I experience Shreveport as a visitor, but one with a window to its past and the nostalgia of going home, and as a daughter reuniting with loved ones. I now frequently bring my Texas family and friends to the "other side" of the great state of Louisiana. It fills me with excitement and pride to show them the magic of the area that I still call home.

Louisiana is nicknamed the Sportsman's Paradise for its abundance of activities for the outdoors lover. The Shreveport area plays its own role in that nickname by offering several lakes for fishing, camping, and water sports. Mix that with 24-hour gaming at riverfront casinos, year-round festivals, a sizzling nightlife, Bossier's Boardwalk with stunning river views, museums, and horse racing, and you have the perfect getaway with something for everyone.

• •

There is no one right way to use this book. If you are visiting Shreveport, my hope is that this book will be a guide as you experience the area's small-town friendliness with big-city amenities. For the local who picks up this book, use it to rediscover Shreveport by becoming a tourist in your hometown. Feel free to start by category, season, or itinerary. The insider tips and activities I share in this book will lead you to the best food, entertainment, recreation, culture, history, and shopping Shreveport-Bossier has to offer. I proudly present my book as a love letter to the cities that raised me, *100 Things to Do in Shreveport-Bossier, Louisiana, Before You Die*. Laissez les bons temps rouler! (Let the good times roll!) Follow my family and our travels on Instagram @monicachampagne, on Facebook @ChampagneOnDeck, and at ChampagneOnDeck.com.

~ Monica Dollar Champagne

• •

Shreveport Aquarium

ACKNOWLEDGMENTS

To write this book, I relied on a lifetime of experiences and on those who experienced them with me. These include local friends who helped me scope out new places and hosted me during visits, business owners who opened the doors of their establishments to my family, and those who took the time to proofread draft after draft of this book.

They include Stephen, Clara, and Conley Champagne; Larry, Lauren, Layne, and Brittany Dollar; Sharon Champagne; LeeAnn Hudson, Ann Susman, and business owners, managers, and service staff of the establishments highlighted in this book.

• •

FOOD
AND DRINK

POP
SOME GATOR BITES
AT RALPH & KACOO'S

Ralph & Kacoo's first opened their doors on the banks of the False River Bend of the old Mississippi. They now have several locations in the southeastern United States, including one in Bossier City!

Locals find themselves here when craving the flavors of New Orleans French Quarter cuisine and superb waitstaff service. The fried gator swamp bites and stuffed mushrooms offer an exciting start to any meal.

Mouthwatering dishes such as flavorful crawfish étouffée and cooked-to-perfection flaky lobster are to die for! Wash it all down with a traditional New Orleans libation, the colossal Hurricane! Meals end with a tempting dessert cart where diners can see exactly how their treat will look. Consider the bread pudding. It is one of their most popular selections.

1700 Old Minden Rd., Ste. 141, Bossier City, 318-747-6660
ralphandkacoos.com

TIP
Browse the False River Gift Shop to grab Cajun-themed souvenirs including cookbooks, spices, and real alligator accessories.

GET SPICY
AT CRAWDADDY'S KITCHEN

Slipping through the doors of Crawdaddy's Kitchen gives you the feeling of being transported directly onto the banks of a southern Louisiana bayou. If you did not know better, you might think someone was out back wrestling a gator for your dinner.

The Louisiana-themed rustic decor and the friendly company are as much fun as the food. Do not be surprised if by the end of the meal you are BFFs with the patrons at the next table.

Crawdaddy's Kitchen has been voted one of the best places to get crawfish in the state. Order crawdads in a gumbo, étouffée, or come sit a spell while you work your way through a platter of boiled mudbugs. They also have other seafood favorites such as fried alligator, boudin balls, fried shrimp, mahi-mahi, and oysters.

9370 Mansfield Rd., Shreveport, 318-688-7532
crawdaddyskitchen.com

TIP
Come during the Mardi Gras season and take home your very own king cake.

INDULGE IN STRAWBERRY ICEBOX PIE
AT STRAWN'S EAT SHOP

Strawn's Eat Shop opened in 1944 across the street from the beautiful, historic Centenary College of Louisiana. Every local knows that this is the best place for pie in Shreveport, but their notoriety extends beyond city lines, having been featured in numerous publications such as *Southern Living* magazine and on the Food Network.

Their buttery crusted icebox pies come in strawberry, chocolate, coconut, banana, butterscotch, and peach and are covered with a homemade whipped topping. Opening at 6 a.m., Strawn's Eat Shop also serves traditional breakfast, omelets, loaded pancakes, and waffles all day.

Other menu options include southern diner staples such as burgers, lightly breaded chicken fried steak, beef tips, and meat loaf. The energetic atmosphere and historical, quirky cartoon murals make this a fun stop on any tourist's itinerary.

125 E Kings Hwy., Shreveport, 318-868-0634
facebook.com/strawnseatshop

TIP
Order a full Strawn's icebox pie to take to your next family gathering. You will be the hit of the party!

SIP
A HAPPY-HOUR
MARGARITA
AT SUPERIOR GRILL

Forty years in business, Superior is known by locals as the happy-hour place to be. The large Styrofoam margarita happy-hour cups paired with top-notch chips and salsa are a familiar sight to those looking to get the party started.

The closed patio is first come, first served, and if you do not come first, you may miss getting a table. It is common to see large parties gathered on the patio to celebrate a special occasion.

On weekends, these patio parties go late with live music and margarita-inspired dancing. It is not just 20-somethings on the dance floor. Ages 5 to 75 can be seen cutting a rug on any Saturday night. For dinner, try Superior's sizzling fajitas, shrimp tacos, or queso flameado.

6123 Line Ave., Shreveport, 318-869-3243
shreveport.superiorgrill.com

TIP
If you are in the mood for a somewhat quieter dining experience, wait for an inside table.

EXPERIENCE CHICAGO-STYLE LUXURY
AT SUPERIOR'S STEAKHOUSE

Superior's Steakhouse is Shreveport's swanky, luxury steak house complete with live piano music and handcrafted cocktails. Mingle in the bar sipping one of the hundreds of international bourbons they offer or find your perfect wine from a list of more than 400 international labels.

The dining rooms are lovely and oozing with class. One even has a fireplace, a rarity in Shreveport restaurants, that really completes the ambiance of sophistication. When the weather allows, open-air and patio dining are also options. In addition to the steaks, some menu favorites include the meat loaf, Louisiana crawfish corn bread, brussels sprouts, and bananas foster prepared tableside. Whether celebrating a birthday, anniversary, college graduation, or simply wanting to socialize in "the place to be seen" bar, Superior's Steakhouse has you covered.

855 Pierremont Rd., Ste. 120, Shreveport, 318-219-4123
superiorssteakhouse.com

TIP
Take advantage of their lunch specials to get the same quality meals at more affordable prices.

LEAVE A KNICKKNACK
AT HERBY-K'S

Referring to themselves as a "classic hole-in-the-wall," Herby-K's has been feeding Shreveport locals since the 1930s. The surrounding abandoned buildings leave a hint of a vital past, but now the area might make you think twice before entering the restaurant. Go ahead and walk through the doors to immediately feel connected to Shreveport's past. The walls are covered with newspaper and magazine articles praising the establishment.

The shelves are cluttered with souvenirs left by guests. As far as food goes, their most popular dish is the Shrimp Buster with its unbelievably large butterflied fried shrimp. It's good, but do not overlook some of the other fabulous menu items including gumbo, burgers, and catfish Chesapeake. Ask if you do not see the Chesapeake on the menu.

1833 Pierre Ave., Shreveport, 318-424-2724
facebook.com/herbyks

TIP
Call ahead if you plan to order the oysters.

ANOTHER GREAT CATCH FOR CATFISH
Jan's River Restaurant
7675 W 70th St., Shreveport, 318-938-5026
janscatfish.com

GRAB A BITE TO EAT
WHILE TOURING DOWNTOWN SHREVEPORT

Downtown Shreveport is full of history and character. Once you have worked up an appetite from all the sightseeing the area has to offer, fuel up at one of the unique Texas Street restaurants. Four eateries you will not want to miss are: the Blind Tiger, Noble Savage Tavern, the Missing Link, and Abby Singer's Bistro.

The Blind Tiger has all your Cajun favorites. Noble Savage Tavern offers a towering muffaletta you have to see to believe and live music. At the Missing Link, you will find hot dogs with limitless toppings. Abby Singer's is on the second floor of the Robinson Film Center, a theater specializing in classic, foreign, and independent films. They have a lovely balcony overlooking Texas Street where you can relish a savory cheese board and specialty cocktails.

The Blind Tiger
120 Texas St.
Shreveport, 318-226-8747
facebook.com/profile.
php?id=100034443145960

The Missing Link
504 Texas St., Ste. 100
Shreveport, 318-751-5820
facebook.com/
themissinglinkfoodservices

Noble Savage Tavern
417 Texas St.
Shreveport, 318-828-2619
thenoblesavageshreveport.com

Abby Singer's Bistro
617 Texas St.
Shreveport, 318-459-4122
robinsonfilmcenter.org/
abby-singers-bistro

GET SAUCY
AT MONJUNIS

If you have a hankering for Italian food, make a stop at one of the locally owned and operated Monjunis restaurants. The funky decor with a sea of grapes hanging from the ceiling gives the restaurant a cozy feeling with a classic diner vibe.

This is the place for comfort food lovers who like their pasta drowning in Louisiana southern sweet marinara sauce! Start with the Cajun shrimp toast or cheesy bread appetizer to dip in that sweet sauce. For your main course, consider ordering the twice-baked lasagna, spaghetti with a giant meatball, or the muffaletta.

The portions are large. Most people will have plenty to take home for a second meal. The refreshing mint tea is a customer favorite for washing down the meal and the Italian creme cake for dessert does not disappoint.

Monjunis on Louisiana Ave.
1315 Louisiana Ave., Shreveport
318-227-0847
facebook.com/og.monjunis

Monjunis Italian Café and Grocery
7601 Youree Dr., Shreveport
318-797-9999
mymonjunis.com

TIP
If you opt for takeout, bring your dog with you through the drive-through. Monjunis locations are known for passing out treats to four-legged friends.

TRY WORLD-FAMOUS CRAB CLAWS
AT ERNEST'S ORLEANS

Visit Ernest's Orleans Restaurant and Cocktail Lounge for an old-world dining experience consisting of steak, seafood, or Italian cuisine. Chef Ernest has become an icon in the Shreveport community. He has made a name for himself through the welcoming environment he creates in his restaurant, his community involvement, and his dedication to a sophisticated retro dining experience.

The award-winning crab claws are a must-order, and you will love sopping up the flavorful oil, vinegar, and herbs with your roll as you finish every morsel. A few local favorite main dish recommendations include the crab meat Orleans, spaghetti and meatballs, and the filet mignon.

Some preparation takes place tableside, such as loading up your baked potato or crafting a decadent flaming dessert. For dessert, order the Cherries Jubilee or Bananas Foster.

1610 Spring St., Shreveport, 318-226-1325
ernestsorleans.com

TIP
Request the "old-style, soft rolls" when ordering.

SHUCK
SOME OYSTERS
AT THE OYSTER BAR AND GRILLE

The Oyster Bar and Grille's big blue awning on the corner of Line and Pierremont has been a Shreveport staple for over 15 years. It covers an outdoor dining patio that is often crowded with locals enjoying lunch, happy hour, or dinner.

Their fresh Louisiana oysters come on the half shell, mesquite grilled, barbecued, or grilled with parmesan cheese and champagne. The champagne oysters are one of the most popular menu items, but their menu expands well beyond oysters. Other items include a wide variety of seafood dishes, po'boys so big you will want to share, juicy burgers, and mouthwatering margaritas. No matter what you decide to order from the robust menu, be sure to ask for a side of the homemade house dressing for dipping!

Go ahead and give the Oyster Bar a try. You just might be one of the lucky ones who leave with a pearl as a lagniappe (Cajun French for something extra)!

855 Pierremont Rd., Ste. 157, Shreveport, 318-213-6978
oysterbarandgrille.com

A FINE-DINING OYSTER BAR
The Pearl Shreveport
6871 Fern Ave., Shreveport, 318-670-7920
thepearlshreveport.com

FEAST UPON SUSHI AND SASHIMI
AT SUSHI GEN

Sushi Gen is the perfect place to impress your boo (Cajun slang for your honey) with high-quality sushi and sashimi. They offer a wide variety of Japanese dishes and a hibachi grill for customers who want to experience this traditional Japanese cooking style first-hand.

Popular appetizers include the Avocado Bomb and the Heart Attack. The Ahi Tower from the specialty menu or a bento box from the grill are also top sellers. Since you are in Louisiana, be sure to add an LSU Tower or the Shreveport Roll to your order. Sushi Gen is sure to satisfy your cravings with its fresh ingredients and traditional recipes.

2300 Airline Dr., Bossier City, 318-584-7320
6607 Line Ave., Shreveport, 318-219-7979
sushigensb.com

TASTE SICILY
AT CHIANTI

Experience the romantic and mellow atmosphere of old-school Italian cuisine at Chianti. Since its opening 35 years ago, Chianti has been serving some of the finest Italian dishes in the area.

The restaurant also features the Green Room, where local musicians play soft piano music, and a vintage wine bar with an extensive selection of wines. For dinner, you cannot go wrong with the Farfalle Con Gamberetti Alfredo or Chianti's signature dish, the Scaloppini Al Limone, made with veal. The German Chocolate Mousse Cake or Chocolate Mousse Brule' are crowd favorites for dessert.

Whether you are looking for a romantic dinner or just want some classy Italian food, Chianti is sure to provide you with an unforgettable experience.

6535 Line Ave., Shreveport, 318-868-8866
chiantirestaurant.net

ENJOY AUTHENTIC MEXICAN FOOD
AT EL PATIO MEXICAN GRILL

El Patio Mexican Grill is a family-owned restaurant that has been serving authentic Mexican food in Louisiana for over 20 years. In 2018, locals rejoiced when a location opened in Shreveport. They celebrated again in 2022 when another location popped up in the hopping East Bank District of Bossier City.

As the name implies, El Patio takes pride in their patio dining. The Bossier City location has an especially extensive patio, making it a perfect gathering place for large parties. The menu items at El Patio are based on generational family recipes. A favorite is the camarones con queso. Order it with caramelized onions for a flavor explosion! They even offer vegetarian options for those who prefer a meat-free meal.

707 Barksdale Blvd., Bossier City, 318-459-6171

9448 Forbing Rd., Shreveport, 318-626-5849
elpatiomexicangrill.com/

TIP
Like it hot? Tell the waiter your heat preference and they will make your meal extra spicy.

OTHER OUTSTANDING MEXICAN RESTAURANTS

El Jimador Supremo Mexican Cuisine
750 Shreveport Barksdale Hwy., Shreveport, 318-861-2001
eljimadorsupremo.com

El Jimador Mexican Grill
2711 Alkay Dr., Shreveport, 318-686-9199
eljimadorcantina.com

Silver Star Cantina
3015 E Texas St., Bossier City, 318-584-7446
silverstarcantina.com

Ki' Mexico
3839 Gilbert Dr., Shreveport, 318-861-5941
facebook.com/kimexico

Cantina Laredo
6535 Youree Dr., Ste. 401, Shreveport, 318-798-6363
cantinalaredo.com/location/shreveport-louisiana

Monzon's Cantina & Grill
2091 Stockwell Rd., Bossier City, 318-562-3359
facebook.com/profile.php?id=100066900551614

EAT GULF OF MEXICO CRAWFISH AND SHRIMP
AT FRANK'S LOUISIANA KITCHEN

Frank's Louisiana Kitchen is a gastronomic sanctuary right within the charming Provenance neighborhood. This dining destination embodies a true Louisiana spirit. Since its inception in late May 2017, Frank's has been delivering an authentic experience, where every dish is a labor of love.

With a commitment to freshness, only the finest seafood, meats, and local produce are used in a thoughtfully prepared true Louisiana fashion. With reverence for tradition, they butcher their own meat and fish, meticulously create boudin and andouille sausage, and cure their own bacon.

They exclusively use succulent Louisiana coast crawfish and shrimp, while their po'boys and bread pudding feature Leidenheimer French bread sourced from New Orleans. The flavors extend to the bar, where expert bartenders concoct classic cocktails and innovative FLK originals that guarantee to "pass a good time."

1023 Provenance Pl. Blvd., Ste. 200, Shreveport, 318-688-3535
frankslakitchen.com

TIP
Frank's also has a wood-fired Pizza Napoletana on Fern Avenue that serves scratch-made pizzas, outstanding steak, and seafood selections.

GO GREEK
AT ATHENA'S GREEK & LEBANESE GRILL

Athena's Greek & Lebanese Grill is a family-owned Mediterranean restaurant located on Line Avenue. They serve a wide variety of traditional Greek and Lebanese dishes, including gyros, mouthwatering grilled lamb chops, and a variety of kebabs.

Warning: the dipping sauce here is out of this world. The Hummus Deluxe with seasoned ground beef or the creamy Grecian Tzatziki dip with warm pita bread makes a delicious appetizer or side dish. They also have an entire menu section dedicated to vegetarian options.

Additionally, Athena's offers a unique experience with their indoor hookah lounge where guests can sip Turkish coffee or tea while smoking flavored tobacco. Want a sweeter end to your meal? Try the elegant and richly layered tiramisu. Come experience the flavors of Greece and Lebanon at Athena's Greek & Lebanese Grill!

6030 Line Ave., 318-869-4260
athenashreveport.com

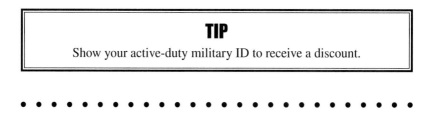

TIP

Show your active-duty military ID to receive a discount.

ORDER STUFFED SHRIMP
AT ORLANDEAUX'S CAFÉ OR
EDDIE'S SEAFOOD AND SOULFOOD

Two of the oldest African American family-owned restaurants can be found in Shreveport. Orlandeaux's Café, located on Cross Lake, has been recognized as the oldest continuously operating African American family-owned restaurant in the United States. They have been serving up delicious Creole recipes passed down for five generations since 1921. Eddie's Seafood and Soulfood Restaurant boasts being the oldest in northwest Louisiana, having never changed its name or location since 1978.

Both serve irresistible, southern soul food and Creole cuisine. At Orlandeaux's, try the boudin balls, spicy alligator balls, gizzards, or Shreveport-style extra stuffed shrimp. When visiting Eddie's, don't pass up the cheesy stuffed shrimp with their one of a kind tarter sauce. Both restaurants' chefs and dishes have received numerous accolades and awards from competitions, magazines, and media outlets.

Orlandeaux's Café
5301 S Lakeshore Dr., Shreveport, 318-688-7777
orlandeauxs.com

Eddie's Seafood and Soulfood Restaurant
1956 Hollywood Ave., Shreveport, 318-631-9082
facebook.com/eddiesstuffedshrimp

FOOD FESTIVALS FOR LOCAL CUISINE

Battle of the Gumbo Gladiators
900 Jordan St., Ste. 102, Shreveport, 318-425-4413
gumbogladiators.com

Crawfest
3901 Fairfield Ave., Shreveport
shreveportevent.com/events/crawfest

318 Restaurant Week
318-222-9391
facebook.com/318restaurantweek

Shreveport Bossier Black Restaurant Week
shreveportblackrestaurantweek.com

WARM YOUR SOUL
AT FAT CALF BRASSERIE

Fat Calf Brasserie is a neighborhood establishment in the Highland community, serving French-inspired Southern cuisine. They pride themselves in creating culinary works of art using locally sourced foods from nearby farmers and suppliers.

Fat Calf offers a variety of fine wines, craft beers, signature cocktails, and mocktails that pair perfectly with their delicious dishes. For an appetizer, do not miss the flash-fried brussels sprouts or Five-Spice Pork Belly "Burnt Ends." Then, try the perfectly crispy duck entrée, and finish off with a surprising butterscotch pudding.

If you are looking to celebrate a special occasion, consider their Chef's Table experience. They will craft a unique dining experience just for your group that includes six courses and wine pairings.

3030 Creswell Ave., Shreveport, 318-351-2253
fatcalfbrasserie.com

TIP
The owners also host an underground supper club called 2nd Act. Message them through their Facebook page to be informed when these pop up.

SPIKE YOUR COFFEE
AT ANOTHER BROKEN EGG CAFE

If you are looking for a truly upscale brunch experience, then try Another Broken Egg Cafe in Shreveport or Bossier. The restaurant's menu features a wide selection of unique breakfast, brunch, and lunch options.

From cheesy grits loaded with shrimp, to flavorful omelets, to Strawberry Pound Cake French Toast, you will find something to please everyone's palate. Toast the day with a classic mimosa or have one your way with a variety of options. Who would not want to try a one-of-a-kind lemon and blueberry or apple pie flavor?

They do not just stop with mimosas; the restaurant offers a full bar with an immense variety of specialty cocktails, Bloody Marys, and spiked coffees. For the serious bruncher, this resort-like café is a fantastic way to start your day's itinerary.

3107 Airline Dr., Ste. 300, Bossier City, 318-402-0240
855 Pierremont Rd., Ste. 132, 318-865-1124
anotherbrokenegg.com

APPRECIATE A GRAND PIANIST FINE-DINING ATMOSPHERE
AT 2 JOHNS

Visit 2 Johns Steak & Seafood for an evening full of class, superb local artistry, a grand pianist, and a fine-dining atmosphere. Imagine a white tablecloth steak dinner, a candlelit room, mellow music, and a sommelier offering the perfect glass of red.

The cooked-to-perfection steak is the highlight of the show, but the wide variety of chicken and seafood options are also to die for. The steak au poivre has made a name for itself in Bossier City; however, if seafood is more your style, try the cast-iron-blackened salmon topped with mango chutney.

As you dine, the perfect lighting, the tunes of the ivory keys, and the inviting atmosphere will draw you in, making the evening unforgettable.

2151 Airline Dr., Ste. 1500, Bossier City, 318-841-5646
2johnsrestaurant.com

DINE IN
AN ELEGANT, HISTORIC
VICTORIAN HOME
AT THE MABRY HOUSE

Slow down and take joy in the elegance of a bygone era at one of Shreveport's premier fine-dining restaurants. Here, you can have a candlelit dinner in a dignified Victorian house built in the 1900s.

Start your meal with a creamy crawfish cheesecake appetizer, a sweet chili-glazed cashew lobster tail, or roasted tomato gouda soup. Choose from savory entrée selections such as crab cakes, duck, red snapper, or Argentina rib eye. End the meal with out-of-this-world classic bread pudding.

The menu changes regularly, but the food is always prepared and presented in an artistic way that will take you back to the grandeur of the past. Come and dine in this historic home and be whisked away to another time.

1540 Irving Pl., Shreveport, 318-227-1121
facebook.com/profile.php?id=100063581832093

TIP
Call and make a Chef's Table reservation for a special unique tasting menu presented by the executive chef himself.

SING, DANCE, AND DINE
AT NICKY'S MEXICAN RESTAURANT

Nicky's Mexican Restaurant has several locations in Shreveport-Bossier. Two of the locations have nightclubs, and the Viking Drive location has live music and karaoke. All serve fabulous authentic southwestern Mexican food. Nicky's Mexican Restaurants are the perfect place for a night out with friends and family.

With their lively atmosphere, you can dance the night away at their Mambo Bongo Coco Loco tropical salsa club or at their more formal Flamingo Salsa Ballroom. The restaurants also offer an excellent selection of Mexican dishes such as crawfish enchiladas and strong margaritas that are sure to help you let loose on the dance floor or hit the karaoke mic.

Nicky's friendly staff, tasty food, and great entertainment makes for a spicy way to end the day.

TIP
Check the entertainment schedule on their website or call ahead for the current weekly events.

SELECT A BOTTLE
FROM THE DEEPEST WINE CELLAR IN NORTH LOUISIANA AT LUCKY PALACE

Voted one of the top 100 Chinese restaurants in the country, Lucky Palace has been delighting guests with gourmet meals and a diversified selection of wines for over 25 years.

To access the restaurant, you must enter through the lobby of a weathered, budget-priced, one-story motel. Walking from the fluorescent-lit lobby of the rent-by-the-week motel through the doors to the white-tablecloth, cozy dining room gives the feeling of being transported to another land. Some of the favorite menu items include duck on scallion pancake, hot and sour soup, Mongolian beef, crispy shrimp and scallops, David's prawns, and Cantonese T-bone.

In addition to award-winning food, Lucky Palace boasts a world-renowned wine list that has earned a semifinalist spot in the James Beard Foundation's Outstanding Wine Programs Awards.

750 Diamond Jacks Blvd., Bossier City, 318-752-1888
theluckypalace.com

TIP
Make a reservation for the highly sought-after lazy Susan table for your family-style meal.

SLURP
SOME BOUGIE NOODLES
AT GHOST RAMEN

This isn't your college cup 'o ramen! What started as a late-night food truck has now morphed into an extremely well-received brick-and-mortar lunch spot favorite. Ghost Ramen has quickly risen in popularity by serving ramen noodle dishes so innovative that all your preconceived notions of the dish will disappear.

Their bowls start with a Cajun spicy broth that bathes the scratch-made noodles. Next, hearty fresh ingredients are piled high on top. These toppings include everything from the perfect soft-boiled egg to veggies, chicken, pork, shrimp, and crawfish. The chefs have masterly crossed the nuances of classic Japanese ramen with the daring flavors of Louisiana-inspired cuisine.

Shreveport-Bossier has gone wild for this surprising cuisine mixture for reasons you have to try for yourself to comprehend.

729 Jordan St., Shreveport, 318-510-6621
facebook.com/profile.php?id=100041691109667

ANOTHER NOODLE HOUSE
Hokkaido Ramen House
7503 Youree Dr., Shreveport, 318-828-1409
hokkaidoramen.life

COOL OFF
WITH A SWEET TREAT

SBC offers specialty dessert shops where the menu items are as pretty as they are tasty. In the Eastbank District, look for the Sugar Sheaux with its wide selection of cakes or Streetcar Station for New Orleans–style shaved ice and ice cream.

For rolled ice cream, check out Yum Yum Dessert Bar on East Kings Highway. If you prefer yogurt over ice cream, head over to Counter Culture, "Home of the Humphrey." You can order their signature yogurt parfait at one of their several locations.

On Line Avenue in Shreveport, you can find Sweetport, a neighborhood ice cream parlor with treats so gorgeous you will think twice about eating them. At the Louisiana Boardwalk Outlets in Bossier City, stop by the Chocolate Crocodile and ask for the Monster Croc!

SWEET TREATS IN SHREVEPORT-BOSSIER

Sugar Sheaux
507 Barksdale Blvd., Bossier City, 318-415-6693
sugarsheaux.com

Streetcar Station
409 Barksdale Blvd., Bossier City
facebook.com/streetcarstation

Yum Yum Dessert Bar
504 E Kings Hwy., Shreveport, 318-996-1055
facebook.com/yumyumdessertbar

Counter Culture
6360 Youree Dr., Ste. A-2, Shreveport, 318-212-1616
eatcounterculture.com

The Chocolate Crocodile
460 Boardwalk Blvd., Bossier City, 318-742-3316
thechocolatecrocodile.com

Buttercups Cupcakes
6535 Youree Dr., Ste. 207, Shreveport, 318-797-6696
ilovebuttercups.com

Crumbl Cookies
7020 Youree Dr., Ste. F, Shreveport, 318-230-7776
crumblcookies.com/layouree

Sweetport
3301 Line Ave., Shreveport, 318-779-1674
facebook.com/sweetporticecream

PINCH A TAIL
AT SHANE'S SEAFOOD & BARBQ

The flavors of Southern Louisiana come alive in every bite at Shane's Seafood & BarBQ! There are several locations to choose from. Bossier has three restaurants and Shreveport has four including the original seasonal Acadian Crawfish stand.

Since its humble beginnings in 1994 as a small, boiled-crawfish hut on Mansfield Road, Shane's has grown to become a local favorite. They specialize in serving up mouthwatering fried catfish, tender barbecue, and, of course, perfectly boiled crawfish. But that is not all: Shane's also offers an authentic taste of Louisiana with their Zwolle tamales and Natchitoches meat pies, along with crispy fried green tomatoes.

More surprisingly, Shane's offers a wide selection of fruit smoothies, power smoothies, and yogurt smoothies, perfect for sipping on a warm Louisiana day.

9133 Mansfield Rd., Shreveport, 318-687-3195
(Only open during crawfish season)
shanesseafood.com

TIP
For those on the go, Shane's offers a convenient drive-through option.

OTHER SHANE'S LOCATIONS

4200 Airline Dr., Bossier City, 318-808-8646

4726 E Texas St., Bossier City, 318-742-8112

5914 Youree Dr., Shreveport, 318-865-6088

9176 Mansfield Rd., Shreveport, 318-687-5015

5750 N Market St., Shreveport, 318-929-0001

5480 Barksdale Blvd., Bossier City, 318-765-7626

UNWIND
AT FLYING HEART BREWING AND PUB

Flying Heart Brewing and Pub is an excellent place to gather with friends, family, and your dog! This hip restaurant and bar is in a renovated historic fire station and offers craft beer and pizza. If you find that all the selections make you feel dizzy, the Louisiana Amber Beer is a suitable place to start.

Feeling creative? You can create your own pizza! The dough is vegan friendly, and they have gluten-free cauliflower crust options as well. Plus, they are child and dog friendly so you can bring the whole family along. They have outdoor seating and cornhole boards for entertainment while you wait for your food. Most Sundays you can even hear live music in their beer garden.

700 Barksdale Blvd., Bossier City, 318-584-7039
flyingheartbrewing.com

MORE HOPPING BREWERIES AND FESTIVALS

Great Raft Brewing
1251 Dalzell St., Shreveport, 318-734-9881
greatraftbrewing.com

The Seventh Tap
2640 Linwood Ave., Shreveport, 318-754-4471
theseventhtap.com

ARTini
8000 E Texas St., Bossier City, 318-741-8310
bossierarts.org/artini/artini-2019

Cork
101 Crockett St., Shreveport, 318-424-4000
redriverrevel.com/cork

SAVOR NEW ORLEANS–STYLE COOKING
AT COPELAND'S OF NEW ORLEANS

Copeland's of New Orleans in Shreveport, Louisiana, is a culinary gem that brings the full flavors of the Big Easy to North Louisiana. This cultural restaurant offers a tantalizing fusion of Cajun and Creole, combined with warm Southern hospitality.

Flip over their eggplant pirogue, jambalaya pasta, or rib eye steak, or savor their signature blackened catfish with mashed sweet potatoes, a true Southern delicacy. Seafood lovers cannot miss the impressive extra-large seafood platter, piled high with popcorn shrimp, catfish strips, crab cake, and beer-battered french fries.

To end the meal, Copeland's of New Orleans is renowned for their exquisite cheesecakes, a heavenly treat that is not to be missed. Many have been known to order an entire cheesecake to take home.

1665 E Bert Kouns Industrial Loop, Shreveport, 318-797-0143
copelandsofneworleans.com

TIP
Go to Copeland's on a Sunday morning for their hearty brunch spread.

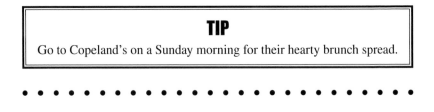

SNAG A DRIVE-THROUGH DAIQUIRI
AT DAIQUIRI EXPRESS

Cruising through a drive-through daiquiri spot in Shreveport is quite amusing for most out of state visitors. By simply placing a piece of tape over the straw hole on these styrofoam cups, they are considered sealed. As soon as the tape is removed, it is violating open-container laws. The Daiquiri Express locations in Shreve City and on Youree Drive both offer this drive-through option. So, go ahead and grab a brightly colored, extra-strong, slushy concoction with a name like Wild Screw, Cajun Curse, or N'walins Mudslide. Remember to enjoy responsibility and keep the tape in place until you get home to comply with local laws. With excellent daily specials like buy one get one free, and over 150 different flavors to choose from, Daiquiri Express just "hits different."

1205 Shreveport Barksdale Hwy., Shreveport, 318-869-2220
8620 Youree Dr. Ste. A, Shreveport, 318-797-1516
daiquiriexpressla.com

Red River Revel

MUSIC
AND ENTERTAINMENT

PLACE A BET
AT A RIVERBOAT CASINO

The sounds of coins clinking, people cheering, and slot machines ringing are commonplace for Shreveport-Bossier's riverboat casinos in Louisiana.

Bally's, Horseshoe, Boomtown, Margaritaville, and Sam's Town casinos all house several levels of popular casino games, from slots to table games, providing a 24-hour full-action experience. These casinos also offer some of the best eats in the area including 1800° Prime Steakhouse, Jack Binion's Steakhouse, Casa di Amici Charcuterie and Wine Bar, and Jimmy's Seafood & Steak.

Additionally, you can find lively entertainment at these establishments such as the 1931 lounge at the Horseshoe Casino or the Allure Ultra lounge at Bally's. If horse racing is more your speed, Louisiana Downs Casino & Racetrack is a popular destination with its renowned Super Derby attracting top-notch horses and jockeys from around the country.

FIVE RIVERBOAT CASINOS

Bally's Shreveport
451 Clyde Fant Pkwy., Shreveport, 318-220-0711
casinos.ballys.com/shreveport

Horseshoe Casino
711 Horseshoe Blvd., Bossier City, 318-742-0711
caesars.com/horseshoe-bossier-city

Boomtown
300 Riverside Dr., Bossier City, 318-746-0711
boomtownbossier.com

Margaritaville
777 Margaritaville Way, Bossier City, 318-698-7177
margaritavillebossiercity.com

Sam's Town
315 Clyde Fant Pkwy., Shreveport, 318-424-7777
samstownshreveport.boydgaming.com

VISIT THE LARGEST PARK
DEDICATED TO ROSES AT THE AMERICAN ROSE CENTER

The American Rose Center is the largest park in the United States dedicated solely to roses. The 118-acre wooded tract situated conveniently at Exit 5 on Interstate 20, between Shreveport and the Texas border displays their impressive variety.

As you explore, you will also come across an array of companion plants, enchanting sculptures, and elegant fountains, including the picturesque Dudley Watkins Reflection Pool. Families can often be found taking photos among the gorgeous plants, playing in the children's area, hiking, or picnicking.

This extraordinary park proudly serves as the national headquarters of the American Rose Society, a renowned organization with a 125-year history. Engulf yourself in the beauty of America's national floral emblem and experience the timeless allure of these cherished flowers.

8877 Jefferson Paige Rd., Shreveport, 318-938-5402
rose.org/visit-public-gardens

TIP
Visit the day after Thanksgiving through the weekend before Christmas for the annual Christmas in Roseland when the gardens are transformed into a whimsical wonderland of twinkling lights and holiday-themed activities and music.

WITNESS THE MAGIC
OF THE BAKOWSKI BRIDGE OF LIGHTS AT GLO FEST

As the sun sets, visit the Bakowski Bridge of Lights, a marvelous art installation on the iconic Texas Street Bridge. Every evening the bridge transforms into a mesmerizing canvas, showcasing a symphony of colors, patterns, and animations of LED lights that cast a reflection on the tranquil waters below.

The first Friday of every month, the Shreveport Regional Arts Council ramps up the show with Glo Fest. This free festival starts at 7 p.m. and goes until 10 p.m. Each event displays a unique light show accompanied by entrancing music, transforming the Bakowski Bridge of Lights into a breathtaking visual spectacle.

Caddo Parish students partner with the Light It Up Artist Team to design the show. Additionally, Glo Fest offers an arts market, food truck court, and riveting street performances.

601 Clyde Fant Pkwy., Shreveport, 318-673-6500
texasstreetbridge.com

TIP

While in the area, explore the Walk of Stars in the Red River District under the Bakowski Bridge of Lights, east of Commerce Street. Created to honor remarkable individuals from northwest Louisiana, this pathway celebrates their exceptional achievements in various fields, including athletics, music, business, and community service.

CELEBRATE WITH LOCALS
AT FESTIVAL PLAZA

Community parties are a deep rooted part of Louisiana culture. Located on the banks of the Red River, Festival Plaza is home to several major community events. The Plaza's signature blue tower is an iconic landmark that welcomes locals and visitors alike to come and join in the celebrations. With two large pavilions spanning over 1,000 square meters each, Festival Plaza is the go to place for outdoor concerts and other events all year long. For example, May brings in MudBug Madness and its quirky crawfish calling contest. Visit in June for the Let The Good Times Roll Festival, a celebration of African American Culture. In October, Shreveport Brew takes over the Plaza with a beer tasting festival that offers over 100 well-crafted beers. The weekend after Thanksgiving, Rockets Over the Red ushers in the holiday season with a magnificent tree lighting ceremony and fireworks show!

101 Crockett St., Shreveport, 318-673-5100
myspar.org/369/festival-plaza

A FEW MORE LOCAL SEASONAL FESTIVALS AND EVENTS

The State Fair of Louisiana
3701 Hudson Ave., Shreveport, 318-635-1361
statefairoflouisiana.com

SBC Zombie Walk
630 Barksdale Blvd., Bossier City, 318-741-8310
bossierarts.org/zombie-walk

DixieMaze Fall Festival
9596 Sentell Rd., Shreveport, 318-703-2870
dixiemaze.com

Pumpkin Shine On Line
3901 Fairfield Ave., Shreveport
southfield-school.org/pumpkin-shine

Red River Balloon Rally
8000 E Texas St., Bossier City
redriverballoonrally.com

Highland Jazz and Blues Festival
700 Columbia St., Shreveport
highlandjazzandblues.org

Geek'd Con
6341 Westport Ave., Shreveport, 318-688-1130
geekdcon.com

Barksdale Defenders of Liberty Air & Space Show
109 Barksdale Blvd., Bossier City, 318-456-1015
defendersoflibertyairshow.com

ASEANA Fall and Spring Festivals
800 Texas Ave., Shreveport, 318-401-8078
facebook.com/asiangardenofshreveport

ROCK OUT
UNDER THE STARS
AT HURRICANE ALLEY

The air buzzes with anticipation every Thursday-Saturday as crowds of people gather at North Louisiana's #1 outdoor concert venue, Hurricane Alley. The stage illuminates, casting a glow that sets the mood for a night of Red Dirt Country, Classic Rock, or Cajun Zydeco music. As the first notes reverberate through the open air, the crowd's energy surges, and inhibitions fade away. Hurricane Alley is the heartbeat of the Eastbank district and just a stroll away from thousands of hotel rooms, including the Horseshoe Casino! They are recognized as one of Louisiana's three open container zones, ensuring that the party never stops. In addition to the weekly live music, Hurricane alley also has special seasonal events and festivals. Check out their event calendar online to stay in touch with all that Hurricane Alley has to offer.

500 Ogilvie St., Bossier City
hurricanealleylive.net

ENTER A KARAOKE CONTEST
AT 1931 LOUNGE

Pass through the sleek grand lobby entrance of the Horseshoe Casino and be greeted by the upbeat 1931 Lounge. At this point you have a choice to make, continue walking towards the ringing sounds of slot machines to test your luck or let the music of the 1931 Lounge lure you to a seat at the wrap-around bar. With free live music Thursday-Saturday nights and delicious cocktails, this bar is one of the more popular places to let loose in Bossier City. The local bands that perform are always top notch and the karaoke is on another level as it draws singers looking to take home a cash prize. Make the night out complete by having dinner beforehand. There are several Horseshoe restaurants right around the corner from the lounge.

711 Horseshoe Blvd., Bossier City, 800-895-0711
caesars.com/horseshoe-bossier-city

ROADTRIP
THE BOOM OR BUST BYWAY

Take off on a road trip adventure along the Boom or Bust Byway in North Louisiana, just 15 minutes from downtown Shreveport on LA 1. This 136-mile self-driving tour unfolds across the parishes of Caddo, Bossier, Webster, and Claiborne. The route offers a blend of local diners, outdoor trails, antique shops, biking paths, historical museums, charming churches, fishing holes, campgrounds, and plantations. You will pass lush farm crops, bayous, fields of wildflowers, and towering trees. See oil field equipment graveyards from the oil industry bust and new facilities reflecting the recent boom of the oil and gas economy. Download the GPS-navigated app for a guided tour through this scenic back road countryside. Try it out to see why the Boom or Bust Byway was named a Southern Travel Treasure by *AAA Southern Traveler* magazine.

boomorbustbyway.com

BET ON A HORSE
AT LOUISIANA DOWNS

The air crackles with excitement as the horses thunder down the track, their hooves echoing the cheers of the crowd. The energy is infectious for both the seasoned bettor and the first-time spectator. The grandstands offer a perfect view of the races, and the atmosphere is charged with anticipation. Beyond the racing action, you can visit the gaming floor, featuring slot machines and table games or enjoy one of the delicious dining options. Live horse racing is year-round at Louisiana Downs, with thoroughbred races captivating audiences from May to September and Quarter Horse racing revving up from January to March. Test your handicapping prowess throughout the year by watching and wagering on live horse races from global racetracks in their state-of-the-art simulcast facilities.

8000 E Texas St., Bossier City, 318-742-5555
ladowns.com

TIP

In December, Louisiana Downs is transformed into the enchanting wonderland of Christmas in the Sky, a biennial black-tie gala that has earned the prestigious title of "Best Gala in the World" by Special Events International Magazine. If you find yourself in the area during that time, consider taking part in this remarkable fundraiser where artistry, generosity, and celebration converge to support the Shreveport arts community.

DESIGN YOUR OWN PRINTS
AT POINT STUDIO ART

Flaunt your individuality by making a one-of-a-kind statement piece. Point Studio Art is a place where you can transform everyday fabric items—such as T-shirts, scarves, and tote bags—into personalized masterpieces. There are several weekly events to choose from. On couples' night, you can hand print your honey's portrait on fabric canvas. On t-shirt night, bring your own tee and let their professional artists guide you through the hand printing process to make your own unique wearable art. If you would like a little more structure to your creation, join them for a theme night where the design is customized and prepared in advance to match your chosen theme. Experimental Prints night allows you to bring any article of clothing to transform into a piece of self-expression.

605 Boardwalk Blvd., Bossier City, 818-928-9205
pointstudioart.com

SUMMON
YOUR INNER FILM CRITIC
AT PRIZE FEST

Since its inception in 2012, Prize Fest has delivered a novel street festival experience in Shreveport. The festival offers an unrivaled celebration of film, music, food, fashion, comedy, and community.

What sets Prize Fest apart is that you are not just a spectator—you have the power to shape the festival's outcome. Watch the films and be a part of the judging process, where the winner walks away with a staggering $50,000 prize, one of the largest for a short film anywhere in the world. Move to the rhythm of the top-voted musicians and take part in choosing the next great chefs.

Witness fashion models strut down the Prize runway in fabulous original designs and be prepared for uproarious laughter courtesy of the region's top comedians.

617 Texas St., Shreveport, 318-213-6437
prizefest.com

JOIN THE PARTY
AT BEARS

At the corner of Fairfield and Southern Avenues, inside the iconic "Alvin Building," Bears stands as Shreveport's beloved neighborhood live music venue, bar, and restaurant.

This establishment is dedicated to fostering good times and providing a late-night environment that locals eagerly anticipate. Bears is a hub for local karaoke stars and avid trivia contestants. From themed karaoke nights to brain-teasing trivia challenges, from exciting bingo sessions to unrestrained indie rock live shows, there is always something happening at Bears. Join the crowd during happy hour, participate in the open jam nights, and sway to the tunes of talented local musicians all while sinking your teeth into an unbelievably juicy burger.

Bears is where diverse walks of life unite, celebrating music, laughter, and community in Shreveport.

1401 Fairfield Ave., Shreveport, 318-606-4267
bearsfairfield.com

TIP
Even though Bears is highlighted here in the Things to Do section, their food is also outstanding.

CHANGE YOUR TUNE
AT LOUISIANA GRANDSTAND

Built in 1925, this historical landmark has received a breath of new life as the intimate musical haven, Louisiana Grandstand. Opening in 2019, they are evolving and enhancing the local music scene in Northwest Louisiana while drawing inspiration from iconic showcases like the historic Louisiana Hayride. Louisiana Grandstand delivers a premium lineup, featuring beloved touring artists from across the nation such as Confederate Railroad, The Randy Rogers Band, and Cody Canada of Cross Canadian Ragweed. They also have charity Opry Nights that are dedicated to nurturing the next wave of talent that will carve their names into Shreveport's storied musical history. The Louisiana Grandstand isn't just a venue; it's a platform for future icons, a place where concerts will become unforgettable chapters in the ongoing saga of Louisiana's musical heritage.

802 Margaret Pl., Shreveport
louisianagrandstand.com

OTHER LIVE MUSIC VENUES
Brookshire Grocery Arena
2000 Brookshire Arena Dr., Bossier City, 318-747-2501
brookshiregroceryarena.com

Shreve Station
400 Crockett St., Shreveport 318-771-2014
shrevestation.com

IMMERSE YOURSELF IN SYMPHONIC SOUNDS
AT THE SHREVEPORT SYMPHONY ORCHESTRA

Established in 1948, the Shreveport Symphony Orchestra is Louisiana's oldest continuously operating professional orchestra. It holds a position of distinction as one of the most esteemed regional orchestras in the United States. Its melodies and harmonies come to life at the renowned Shreveport RiverView Theater from September to May. The symphony performs an assorted composition of musical offerings, ranging from classical masterpieces to seductive pop. Do not miss the opportunity to witness the magic and elegance of the Shreveport Symphony Orchestra, a true testament to the power and beauty of orchestral music.

616 Jordan St., Shreveport, 318-222-7496
shreveportsymphony.com

ANOTHER PERFORMING ARTS EXPERIENCE
Shreveport Metropolitan Ballet
1520 N Hearne Ave., Ste. 116, Shreveport, 318-221-8500
shreveportmetroballet.org

HONOR OUR GREAT NATION
AT FREEDOM FEST

From Memorial Day through July Fourth, KTBS and KPXJ launch Freedom Fest, a campaign that emphasizes the importance of God and country to unite the Ark-La-Tex in a reaffirmation of the principles that have sustained our country throughout history.

The event includes inspiring patriotic messages from local ministers, heartfelt recognition of the sacrifices made by our fellow community members, a life jacket giveaway, an American flag giveaway on Flag Day, free admission to the Louisiana State Exhibit Museum, and more.

Freedom Fest wraps up on July 4 with a huge party at Festival Plaza that includes electrifying concerts; red, white, and blue lights on the Bakowski Bridge; and simultaneous fireworks displays in multiple towns across the Ark-La-Tex.

ktbs.com/freedomfest

CATCH SOME BEADS
AT A MARDI GRAS CELEBRATION

Throw me something, mister! Join the festive spirit and embrace the excitement of Mardi Gras parades and celebrations in Shreveport-Bossier. Louisiana's cultural tradition comes alive as the region delivers a plethora of parties and family-friendly parades.

The festivities kick off in January with the Twelfth Night crowning, where the kings, queens, and royal courts of the area's krewes are revealed to the public. The season continues with a lineup of dazzling balls, fundraisers, tastings, and surprise pop-up parties.

The anticipation grows as the grand parades draw near, overtaking the city with their mesmerizing floats, marching bands, and the colorful beads and trinkets that rain down from the sky. On parade nights, the parties go on all day, so be sure to claim your spot early and take in all that Mardi Gras has to offer.

SIX LOCAL MARDI GRAS KREWES

Krewe of Barkus and Meoux
barkusandmeoux.org

Krewe of Gemini
kreweofgemini.com

Krewe of Highland
thekreweofhighland.org

**Fat Tuesday Children's Parade
of Shreveport & Bossier City**
facebook.com/fattuesdaychildrensparade

Krewe of Sobek
kreweofsobek.org

Krewe of Centaur
kreweofcentaur.org

JAM TO LIVE MUSIC
AT THE EAST BANK
DISTRICT AND PLAZA

Once known as "Old Bossier," this area has undergone a remarkable transformation to become the city's revitalized entertainment district. With several restaurants and bars, live music at Hurricane Alley, an urban park, extensive bike lanes, and a dedicated festival plaza serving as a focal point for community events and gatherings, this district holds immense appeal for both residents and visitors.

Located within half a mile of almost 2,000 hotel rooms, multiple casinos, the Louisiana Boardwalk, and I-20, the East Bank District has quickly emerged as a coveted entertainment jewel in Northwest Louisiana. When visiting the East Bank District, walk through the Cultural District with drink in hand, as it is the only open-container district in North Louisiana and only the second in Louisiana, in addition to Bourbon Street in New Orleans!

615 Barksdale Blvd., Bossier City, 318-741-8310
eastbankmafia.com/venue

TIP
Keep an eye out for murals hidden throughout the Cultural District that tell the history of Bossier City.

A FEW CAN'T-MISS
EASTBANK DISTRICT ESTABLISHMENTS

**The Swamp
at Streetcar Station**
800 Barksdale Blvd.
Bossier City
facebook.com/streetcarsnoballs

BeauxJax Crafthouse
501 Barksdale Blvd.
Bossier City, 318-584-7169
beauxjax.com

Frozen Pirogue
515 Barksdale Blvd.
Bossier City, 318-459-6672
frozenpirogue.com

The L'Italiano Restaurant
701 Barksdale Blvd.
Bossier City, 318-747-7777
thelitalianorestaurant.com

Hoot & Holler Archery
601 Barksdale Blvd.
Bossier City, 318-747-6501
hootnhollerarchery.com

**Flying Heart
Brewing and Pub**
700 Barksdale Blvd.
Bossier City, 318-584-7039
flyingheartbrewing.com

Bayou Axe Throwing Co.
509 Barksdale Blvd.
Bossier City, 318-588-5095
bayouaxe.com

Hurricane Alley
500 Ogilvie St.
Bossier City, 318-584-7169
hurricanealleylive.net

Drunken Monkey Tavern
905 Barksdale Blvd.
Bossier City, 318-550-5202

ESCAPE TO A NEW WORLD
AT A LIVE THEATER PERFORMANCE

There is no shortage of captivating live theater performances in Shreveport-Bossier. The Strand Theatre, an architectural gem, showcases Broadway-style productions and concerts. East Bank Theater offers multifarious performances, from thought-provoking dramas to lighthearted comedies

The Shreveport Little Theatre, one of the oldest continuously producing community theaters in the US, stages classic plays and contemporary works with flair. Marjorie Lyons Playhouse, located at Centenary College, offers cutting-edge performances from aspiring actors and directors, pushing the boundaries of creativity. The BPCC Cavalier Players at Bossier Parish Community College are known for their innovative productions and fresh perspectives.

Built by the Congregation of the First Methodist Church, the Emmett Hook Center is a state-of-the-art facility constructed for concerts, worship services, theatrical productions, seminars, and lectures.

TIP

Enjoy the history of the East Bank Theatre by visiting between productions and asking to view the old jail cells! Left over from when this building once operated as the Bossier City Municipal Building, the original jail cells have been retrofitted into the dressing rooms for actors and performers, with over three decades worth of signatures and autographs by actors, directors, and crew adorning the walls!

OTHER SHREVEPORT-BOSSIER THEATERS

The Strand Theatre
619 Louisiana Ave., Shreveport, 318-226-1481
thestrandtheatre.com

East Bank Theatre
630 Barksdale Blvd., Bossier City, 318-741-8310
bossierarts.org

Shreveport Little Theatre
812 Margaret Pl., Shreveport, 318-424-4439
shreveportlittletheatre.com

Marjorie Lyons Playhouse
2700 Woodlawn Ave., Shreveport, 318-869-5242
centenary.edu/campus-community/marjorie-lyons-playhouse

BPCC Cavalier Players
6220 E Texas St., Bossier City, 318-678-6021
facebook.com/bpcctheatre

Emmett Hook Center
550 Common St., 318-429-6885
emmetthookcenter.org

REWATCH
A CULT CLASSIC
AT THE ROBINSON FILM CENTER

Located in downtown Shreveport, this cultural haven offers an enriching experience for movie enthusiasts and art lovers alike. With its modern theaters and historic charm, the Robinson Film Center presents an eclectic selection of films ranging from classic masterpieces to contemporary indie films.

Their unique screenings, red carpet parties, and film festivals celebrate the diversity of storytelling. The engaging workshops and discussions are designed to foster creativity and dialogue among fellow cinephiles. Special programs such as Date Nights, Friday Night Freakout, and Heels and Reels offer themed movies with a buffet and cash bar. Beyond the silver screen, the center houses a delightful café, Abby Singer's Bistro.

The café serves gourmet treats and beverages that can be enjoyed inside or on the balcony overlooking the historic downtown area.

617 Texas St., Shreveport, 318-459-4122
robinsonfilmcenter.org

HONKY-TONK
THE NIGHT AWAY
AT BIG COUNTRY

Two-step into the nonstop party. Big Country is the ultimate nightclub and country bar experience in Bossier City. On the lower level, flaunt your line-dancing prowess to popular country and top 40 tunes. Need a break from dancing?

Take a wild ride on the mechanical bull, showing off your rodeo skills. Upstairs, get ready to groove to the latest pop and techno hits as you dance the night away on the spacious dance floor. Karaoke weekends are a must for unleashing your inner superstar and enjoying some lively sing-along sessions with friends.

For the appetite you are sure to acquire from all that excitement, their daily, full-service restaurant awaits you with burgers, dogs, fried fish, chicken sandwiches, and pizza.

1003 Gould Dr., Bossier City, 318-584-7218
bigcountrybossier.com

TIP
Do not know how to line dance? No worries! Big Country hosts free line-dancing classes every Friday night.

Bayou Axe Throwing Co.

SPORTS
AND RECREATION

KNOCK DOWN SOME PINS
AT HOLIDAY LANES

Established in 1960, this bowling alley has been a favorite destination for friendly competition and family entertainment. As the oldest operating bowling alley in Louisiana, Holiday Lanes holds a special place in the hearts of locals.

The recent transformation into an Intergalactic Bowling and Arcade experience has taken the excitement to a whole new level with glow-in-the-dark lanes, cosmic-themed graphics, and hypnotic outer space visuals.

Kids love the bumper bowling lanes, ensuring the balls stay out of the gutters and smiles remain on their faces. The Intergalactic Arcade offers more than 50 interactive games for gamers of all ages. Visit on a Friday or Saturday night for Glow Bowl, the thrill of bowling with the lights down low, fantastic music turned up, videos, and special effects lighting that create a party ambiance.

3316 Old Minden Rd., Bossier City, 318-746-7331
bowlholidaylanes.com

START YOUR ENGINE
AT PARTY CENTRAL
FAMILY FUN CENTER

Party Central guarantees a day filled with an impressive range of activities where kids' dreams come true. Get ready for adrenaline-pumping thrills on the go-kart track, where you can put your racing skills to the test.

The arcade offers a plethora of games, from classic favorites to the latest interactive experiences, ensuring endless hours of gaming. Swing for the fences in the batting cages or engage in friendly competition on the bumper boats.

Take on the challenge of the rock-climbing wall or test your precision on the miniature golf course. For an exhilarating adventure, conquer the towering 25-foot super slide or bump your way through the bumper car arena. Younger children will love the kiddie rides designed just for them.

4401 Viking Dr., Bossier City, 318-742-7529
partycentralinfo.com

ANOTHER ARCADE
Island Fun
324 E Boardwalk Blvd., Bossier City, 318-747-8487

THROW AN AXE
AT BAYOU AXE THROWING CO.

Bayou Axe Throwing Co. is Louisiana's premier indoor axe throwing venue. As the state's first dedicated facility, they offer an exciting experience for axe enthusiasts and newcomers alike.

Safety is top priority, and their well-trained team goes the extra mile to ensure all regulations are met. Before you even lay hands on an axe, you will participate in a comprehensive briefing session to familiarize yourself with the rules and safety procedures.

Qualified instructors guide participants one-on-one, teaching the proper throwing technique to hit the target with precision. In addition to axe throwing, they have a broad selection of food and drinks and special events like karaoke nights and ladies nights. Visit Bayou Axe Throwing Co. to get in touch with your inner lumberjack, let off some steam, and start the party.

509 Barksdale Blvd., Bossier City, 318-588-5095
bayouaxe.com

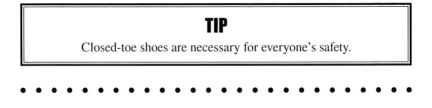

TIP
Closed-toe shoes are necessary for everyone's safety.

TEST YOUR WITS
AT ESCAPE SBC

Calling all Sherlocks. Escape SBC offers a live-action, interactive game and team-building activity that will put your detective skills to the test.

Gather your friends, family, or colleagues and dive into a challenge where you become the hero of your own story. In groups of 2 to 12 players, you will be locked in a room and work together to unravel mysteries, uncover hidden secrets, and solve mind-bending puzzles to accomplish your mission of escaping the room.

With locations in both Shreveport and Bossier City, you have multiple themed rooms to choose from. Each room is uniquely designed, transporting you to a different world and setting the stage for a race against the clock. Do you have what it takes to escape in the nick of time?

8856 Youree Dr., Shreveport
2708 Plantation Dr., Bossier City, 318-564-8668
escapesbc.com

PET UNDERWATER CREATURES
AT THE SHREVEPORT AQUARIUM

The Shreveport Aquarium is a destination for sea animal lovers of all ages. With more than 300 species and 1,000 animals, guests can get up close and personal with a wide range of sea creatures and reptiles, including sharks, seahorses, turtles, and eels.

What makes the Shreveport Aquarium stand out is the opportunity for patrons to hand-feed the stingrays, touch the moon jellies, sea stars, anemones, and more. The aquarium also offers educational opportunities for guests to learn about how these animals adapt and survive in their environment. Kids love the hands-on exhibits such as knot tying, inspecting shark teeth under a microscope, and gem mining.

The friendly staff are always available to help guests make the most of their visit, ensuring a warm, welcoming, and educational atmosphere.

601 Clyde Fant Pkwy., Shreveport, 318-383-0601
shreveportaquarium.com

TIP

Visit anytime during the month of October for Mutiny at Shreveport A-SCAR-ium when the Aquarium transforms into a spooky Pirate themed adventure.

FLY THROUGH THE GALAXY
AT SCI-PORT DISCOVERY CENTER

The Sci-Port Discovery Center is an interactive and educational experience with permanent and rotating awe-inspiring exhibits. In the open-air escape room, the Gallery of Intrigue, players can solve history-based adventures by answering puzzles, riddles, and mysteries using clues found in the gallery.

The museum also boasts an IMAX featuring a 4K laser projection system that provides an immersive cinematic experience like no other. The children's area, PoP, is designed to encourage constructive play, helping children uncover the world around them in a fun and interactive way.

In the planetarium, guests can experience a journey through space through stunning visuals and informative presentations that offer guests the opportunity to ask questions and deepen their understanding of the cosmos.

820 Clyde Fant Pkwy., Shreveport, 318-424-3466
sci-port.org

TIP
Visit during November or December to experience their snow-themed exhibit, SnoPort!

SCALE A WALL
AT A ROCK-CLIMBING GYM

Hidden inside Shreveport Indoor Soccer you can find 318 Climb. In Bossier City off Highway 3, you can find Risen Rock Climbing Gym.

Both are massive rock wall–climbing businesses with opportunities tailored to all skill levels. If you're a new climber, fear not! The gyms have a wide selection of beginner-friendly and kid-friendly routes designed to introduce you to the demanding sport.

You can even enhance your skills by enrolling in private classes. Experienced staff will equip you with the necessary gear and provide expert guidance to prepare you for the ultimate climb. Both facilities offer special happenings such as birthday parties, Nerf Gun parties, Glow Climbs, parents nights out, leagues, toddler time, workshops, fitness classes, and camps.

318 Climb
731 American Way, Shreveport, 318-585-0235
318climb.com

Risen Rock Climbing Gym
1060 Chinaberry Dr., Bossier City, 318-393-1655
risenrockclimbing.com

SPLATTER SOME PAINT
AT OFF LIMITS PAINTBALL

Off Limits Paintball, Louisiana's oldest and largest paintball facility, is just a 30 minute drive from Shreveport-Bossier. With over 50 acres and 13 playing fields, you can enjoy a variety of realistic scenarios and challenges, from urban warfare to jungle survival. Most groups get to experience four or more fields in a single session. Groups of any size are welcome. They will combine groups as needed to make a game. Off Limits Paintball has everything you need to play, including equipment rental, repair, and sales. Concessions and picnic tables are also on site. You can make reservations online or by phone, or just walk in and join the action. Don't miss the Monthly Mixer, where you can meet new friends and play with other paintball enthusiasts.

610 Robinson Rd., Elm Grove 318-987-2696
offlimitspaintball.com

SPOT CHIMPANZEES
IN THEIR FOREST HABITATS

Chimp Haven is right outside of Shreveport in Keithville. They offer a one-of-a-kind experience to those interested in learning about chimpanzees.

As a sanctuary for retired chimpanzees from biomedical research, Chimp Haven provides personalized care for these animals to ensure they can live out their remaining years in a comfortable and stimulating environment. The sanctuary's 200 acres of wide-open woodland spaces are designed entirely for the chimps to roam freely, fill up with fresh fruits and veggies, and live in large families. With special goings-on like Brunch in the Wild, hayrides, and private tours, at Chimp Haven you can expect to experience full chimpanzee discovery.

You can observe the chimps in their natural habitats, learn about their behaviors and veterinary care, and engage with interactive stations that demonstrate life at the sanctuary.

13600 Chimpanzee Pl., Keithville, 318-925-9575
chimphaven.org

TIP
Some experiences are only offered a few times a year and reservations are required.

ZIP-LINE
OVER ALLIGATORS
AT GATORS & FRIENDS

If you are traveling into Shreveport from the west, Gators & Friends is an easy stop off the highway right before you get into town. With over 30 years of experience in the wildlife business, Gators & Friends holds an impressive collection of animals including giant alligators, lemurs, and more than 20 diverse types of exotic animals.

The park also offers daily feeding shows where you can watch the alligators wrestle and leap from the water. For those looking for a more hands-on experience, the exotic animal petting zoo allows patrons to feed and pet the animals in a safe and clean environment.

A highlight for most is the opportunity to hold a baby gator! Additionally, the park features zip lines, go-karts, and an arcade.

11441 US Hwy. 80, Greenwood, 318-938-1199
gatorsandfriends.com

TIP

Availability of animals and attractions varies from day to day. Call ahead if you are hoping to participate in a specific activity or see a certain animal.

BOUNCE
TO NEW HEIGHTS
AT A TRAMPOLINE PARK

When your kids need to burn some energy, there is nothing better than a trampoline park. Shreveport answers that call with Adventure Fun Park, and Bossier does the same with Altitude Trampoline Park.

Jumping alone can entertain the littles for hours, but these parks offer even more than trampolines. Kids can play in foam pits, take on a ninja obstacle course, bounce in air bag pits, shoot some hoops, and battle it out on dodgeball courts.

Get your children off their screens with no complaints by rewarding them with this type of outing. Your kids will have the time of their lives and you will feel good knowing they are improving their cardiovascular health, strengthening muscles, and improving balance and coordination.

Altitude Trampoline Park
2917 Douglas Dr., Bossier City, 318-716-1711
altitudebossier.com/altitude-trampoline-park

Adventure Fun Park
424 Ashley Ridge Blvd., Shreveport 318-606-2367
adventure-shreveport.com

FLOAT THE LAZY RIVER
AT SPLASH KINGDOM OASIS

Any kid who grew up in the Shreveport area is bound to have fond memories of Splash Kingdom Oasis. This sprawling water park offers a respite from the sweltering summer heat.

Bursting with several adrenaline-rushing attractions, this park has seven different towering waterslides that feature steep drops and twisty tunnels. If that is not enough, thrill seekers can also brave the heart-pounding wave pool. For those opting for relaxation, serene cabanas, lounging areas, or the leisurely rotation of the lazy river provide tranquil retreats.

The Kingdom Falls area with dump buckets, spray ground, and small slides is perfect for the little ones. The four-and-a-half-foot-deep activity pool and sand volleyball courts ensure that everyone will find something they will enjoy.

7670 W 70th St., Shreveport, 318-938-5475
splashkingdomwaterpark.com/shreveport-oasis

CAST A LINE
AT AN AREA LAKE

Louisiana is nicknamed the Sportsman's Paradise for good reason. The wildlife and fish are as diverse as the people. The area lakes are part of a series of lakes known as the Great Raft formed from a giant logjam in the 12th century.

Cross Lake, inside the city limits, covers almost 9,000 acres. The largest freshwater lake in the South, Caddo Lake, borders Louisiana and Texas and envelops a massive 25,400 acres.

Just north of Bossier City in Benton, visitors can find Cypress and Black Bayou Lakes. The Cypress Black Bayou Recreation and Water Conservation District offers camping, swimming, marina, fishing piers, and even a small zoo! To the east, Lake Bistineau and Wallace Lake are a fisherman's dream nestled among picturesque cypress trees.

SIX AREA LAKES AND PARKS

**Cypress Black Bayou Recreation
and Water Conservation District**
135 Cypress Park Dr., Benton, 318-965-0007
cypressblackbayou.com

**Wallace Lake/Milton James "Hookie" Cameron
Memorial Park**
10500 Wallace Lake Rd., Shreveport, 318-212-0220
caddo.org/facilities/facility/details/15

**Lake Bistineau
199-101 Pub Camp Rd., Elm Grove**
bossierparishla.gov/experience-bossier-parish/
parish-park-recreation-areas/parish-camp-on-lake-bistineau

Cross Lake/Richard Fleming Park
7919 W Lakeshore Dr., Shreveport, 318-212-0220
caddoparks.org/map/richard-fleming-park

Black Bayou/Noah Tyson Park & Robert L. Nance Park
9300 Mira Myrtis Rd., Rodessa, 318-212-0220
caddoparks.org/map/noah-tyson-park

BIKE OR FISH
AT THE RED RIVER

The Red River joins Shreveport-Bossier and crosses through seven Louisiana parishes. It has become the backdrop of several entertainment spots in Shreveport and Bossier City including casinos, the Louisiana Boardwalk Outlets, Shreveport's Red River District, and the Bakowski Bridge of Lights.

The Red River scenic bicycle trail runs eight miles from Riverview Park in downtown Shreveport to Charles and Marie Hamel Memorial Park near 70th Street. The fishing is excellent on the river. Major bass fishing tournaments take place here thanks to the abundance of three-to-eight-pound largemouths that call it home. Cabin or RV camp at Red River South Marina & Resort and take advantage of their boat ramps and covered slips for easy access to the Red River.

Red River Waterway Commission
5941 Hwy. 1 Bypass, Natchitoches, 318-352-7446
redriverwaterway.com

Red River South Marina & Resort
250 Red River S Marina Rd., Bossier City, 318-747-9545
redriversouthmarinala.com

TIP

Even though people do it, swimming is not recommended in the Red River. The red staining of your clothes will be the least of your worries. The current and the gators are reasons enough to remain on dry land.

PICNIC
AT A LOCAL PARK

Parks can provide free fun, and Shreveport-Bossier has a great collection of them. One gem is the Walter B. Jacobs Memorial Nature Park, a haven for nature and hiking fans.

This lovely park offers scenic trails that wind through woodlands and live animal exhibits. For a more urban park experience visit Caddo Common Park. With its open green spaces, art installations, and interactive features, it serves as a gathering place for community events and outdoor concerts. Eddie D. Jones Park provides a serene escape with its tranquil ambiance, featuring well-maintained gardens and over 20 miles of trails.

Another treasured park, East Kings Highway Park, will charm you with the large and varied population of ducks and geese, where families can feed the birds and take leisurely strolls along the water's edge.

OTHER SHREVEPORT PARKS

Walter B. Jacobs Memorial Nature Park
8012 Blanchard Furrh Rd., Shreveport, 318-929-2806
caddoparks.org/map/walter-b-jacobs-memorial-nature-park

Caddo Common Park
801 Crockett St., Shreveport, 318-673-6537
shrevearts.org/ccpark

Eddie D. Jones Park
8400 Mike Clark Rd., Keithville, 318-210-8388
caddoparks.org/map/eddie-d-jones-park

East Kings Highway Park
1200 E Kings Hwy., Shreveport, 318-673-7727
myspar.org/333/east-kings-highway-duck-pond-park

Riverview Park
601 Clyde Fant Pkwy., Shreveport, 318-673-7727
myspar.org/340/Riverview-Park

ASEANA Asian Gardens
800 Texas Ave., Shreveport, 318-401-8078
facebook.com/asiangardenofshreveport

Betty Virginia Park
3901 Fairfield Ave., Shreveport, 318-673-7727
myspar.org/329/betty-virginia

WATCH A
COLLEGE FOOTBALL GAME
AT THE INDEPENDENCE BOWL

The Independence Bowl, a college football postseason game held annually at Independence Stadium, showcases top-notch collegiate teams battling it out on the gridiron.

Football fans can feel the excitement and passion of the game while being entertained by the electric atmosphere that permeates the stadium. To enhance the game-day experience, take part in the Independence Bowl Coca-Cola Fan Fest. This lively pregame, tailgating celebration takes place near the stadium and offers many entertainment options such as a DJ, corn hole, and inflatables for kids.

The Coca-Cola Fan Fest also joins forces with the ESPN Events Tailgate Tour to provide attendees with complimentary food, exciting prizes, and an abundance of fun-filled activities.

401 Market St., Shreveport, 318-221-0712
radiancetechnologiesindependencebowl.com

EXPLORE ECOSYSTEMS AND WILDLIFE
AT THE RED RIVER
NATIONAL WILDLIFE REFUGE

Visit the Red River National Wildlife Refuge and go on a wildlife-watching or photography adventure to spot a variety of species that call the refuge home.

Keep an eye out for majestic bald eagles, elusive white-tailed deer, and a myriad of waterfowl, wading birds, and songbirds. Relish a peaceful hike in the bottomland hardwood forests, wetlands, and riverbanks.

Additionally, visitors can participate in paddling, hunting, and fishing activities. The refuge provides access to prime fishing spots where you can try your luck at catching a variety of freshwater species. Stop by the refuge's interpretive center, where you can learn about the region's ecology, conservation efforts, and the importance of preserving wildlife habitats. Participate in guided walks, workshops, and informative presentations to deepen your understanding of the refuge's significance.

150 Eagle Bend Point, Bossier City, 318-742-1219
fws.gov/refuge/red-river

CHEER ON THE MUDBUGS HOCKEY TEAM
AT HIRSCH MEMORIAL COLISEUM

Shreveport is home to the Mudbugs, a team in the North American Hockey League (NAHL). The Mudbugs ice hockey team is adored by locals, making it Shreveport's longest-lasting sports franchise.

Entering the area, you will feel the fervent energy from the rowdy fans displaying their unwavering support for the team. You will dig watching the skill and athleticism of the players as they glide across the ice, displaying their prowess.

The fast-paced gameplay, impressive goals, and bone-crunching hits will keep you on the edge of your seat. Even non-hockey fans adore these games. The excitement is infectious, and the crowd really gets involved. These affordable games take place at George's Pond at Hirsch Memorial Coliseum and occasionally offer public ice-skating sessions.

3207 Pershing Blvd., Shreveport, 318-636-7094
mudbugshockey.com

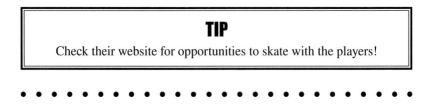

TIP
Check their website for opportunities to skate with the players!

HIT THE LINKS
AT QUERBES PARK GOLF COURSE

As the oldest and most historic active golf course in the area, Querbes Park holds a storied past, having nurtured the talents of golf legends like Hal Sutton and David Toms.

This hallowed ground also once hosted legendary PGA figures Sam Snead and Ben Hogan in a historic exhibition match, further solidifying its significance in the golfing world.

Recent times have seen the revitalization of Querbes Park Golf Course. With a determined focus on the turf, an ambitious agronomic plan has been executed, ensuring the dominance of Bermuda grass throughout the course and cultivating a healthier environment for years ahead. Catering to golfers of all skill levels, Querbes Park offers a welcoming and challenging experience.

3500 Beverly Place, Shreveport, 318-673-7773
spargolf.org

ANOTHER MUNICIPAL GOLF COURSE
The Club at Huntington Park
8300 Pines Rd., Shreveport, 318-673-7765
spargolf.org

PARTICIPATE IN A BIKE TOUR
WITH SOCIAL BIKE RIDES

Socialize, exercise, and see the city all at once with SB Rides. It is perfect for those who do not own bicycles and are looking to explore the area through casual, leisurely cruises.

The tours include scheduled stops at local restaurants and bars, taking you through historic districts to admire the beautiful architecture of Shreveport-Bossier. Glide through the bike-friendly East Bank District in Bossier or pedal along the scenic Downtown Shreveport Riverview Park area, with views of the Red River.

With several routes and tours to choose from at a wide variety of price points, this is a fantastic way to discover hidden gems, meet new people, and experience the local community.

700 Old Minden Rd., Bossier
800 Clyde Fant Pkwy., 318-519-0957
socialbikerides.com

TIP
Bring your own bike and ride for free or for a small donation on their regularly scheduled weekly rides.

PLAY LIKE A PRO
AT SURGE ENTERTAINMENT

Climb, bowl, shoot, swing, game, and eat, all under one roof! This entertainment mecca offers an exhilarating lineup of activities that cater to all ages and interests.

Unleash your competitive spirit with a round of state-of-the-art bowling, complete with innovative scoring systems, huge HD video screens, music, and premium lighting. Experience the thrill of laser tag as you engage in epic battles within multilevel arenas, dodging beams and strategizing with your team. Play arcade games, from classic favorites to the latest 7D interactive experiences and sports simulators.

Do not miss the heart-pounding excitement of their rope course, where you can test your agility and bravery among the sky-high obstacles. The Surge Prime Bistreaux, their on-site restaurant, ensures that you stay fueled for fun with a wide-ranging menu.

2950 E Texas St., Bossier City, 318-678-5895
surgefun.com/locations/bossier-city

TIP
Reserve a private VIP bowling lane for an upgraded experience including a dedicated lane service.

Spring Street Museum,
courtesy of Layne Dollar

CULTURE
AND HISTORY

WALK THE MUSIC LEGENDS LINE
AT THE SHREVEPORT MUNICIPAL AUDITORIUM

Located just west of downtown Shreveport, the Shreveport Municipal Auditorium is a treasured building, celebrated for its art deco construction.

Designed by Samuel Weiner and dedicated to the Soldiers of the Great War in 1929, it initially served as barracks for troops and housed the early aircraft warning system, Radar. However, its true fame came from hosting the groundbreaking program, the Louisiana Hayride, starting in 1948. This weekly showcase catapulted numerous artists to stardom, including legends like Hank Williams, Johnny Cash, and Johnny Horton. Most notably, Elvis Presley made his debut here in 1954.

Today, the auditorium remains a busy venue, hosting family shows, sporting games, and concerts. Recognized as a National Historic Landmark, it continues to reverberate with echoes of music and history.

705 Elvis Presley Ave., 318-841-4000
shreveportmunicipalauditorium.com

TIP

Book a group or private backstage tour of the Municipal Auditorium and hear the music history stories that graced this theater. Additionally, you can email Johnny Wessler at Johnny.Wessler@gmail.com for a personalized Shreveport Cradle of the Stars Music Tour.

BECOME
AN ARTIST FOR A DAY
AT THE RED RIVER REVEL

This popular art and music festival spans nine exciting days, providing a variety of fun family-friendly experiences. Snack on a funnel cake or a Natchitoches meat pie while exploring the works of more than 80 visual artists representing 15 different mediums such as oils, acrylics, sculpture, jewelry, woodwork, glass, and metal.

Delight in the performances of more than 60 artists across multiple genres, creating a lively atmosphere for visitors of all ages. The children's area includes action rides and interactive exhibits, face painting, action sports, a Mock Dig, and the Brookshire's miniature grocery store. With activities catering to everyone, the Red River Arts Festival has been a beloved tradition for over 45 years. Mark your calendars for this October to catch the creativity and culture of this Shreveport tradition.

101 Crockett St., Ste. C, Shreveport, 318-424-4000
redriverrevel.com

TIP
Admission is free during weekdays and only $5 on evenings and weekends.

MAKE SAND ART
AT ARTBREAK

ArtBreak is a much-anticipated spring event that focuses on the student art of all Caddo Parish Schools' students. Visual and performing arts are celebrated and awarded. Enjoy the first-class talent show, poetry readings, music lessons, film screenings, fashion show, culinary competition, and thousands of visual and literary student artworks. Expect to be entertained by the full day lineups of local band, choir, drama, and dance line performances.

One of the biggest hits of the festival for children is the hands-on art activities. Plan to spend some time in this area. It is not unusual for there to be 50 different offerings! The types of kids craft opportunities you can expect are things like sand bottle art, watercolor painting, puppets on a stick, pool noodle caterpillars, and silly hats, to name a few.

801 Crockett St., Shreveport, 318-673-6500
artbreaksb.com

EMBARK ON A PUBLIC ART WORKS SCAVENGER HUNT
AT SHREVEPORT COMMON

From the east end of Shreveport's historic Ledbetter Heights neighborhood to the west edge of downtown, Shreveport Common emerges as a reimagined space after years of neglect, spanning nine blocks of transformative urban renewal.

Recognized on a national scale, it secured the title of "#1 Outstanding Community Development Project in the Nation" by the National Development Council's Academy in Washington, DC. Amid this rejuvenated space, an ensemble of captivating public art flourishes.

The area houses intricate murals that narrate vibrant stories, while the towering 20-foot "Artistrees," illuminated by both sun and LEDs, stand as awe-inspiring landmarks day and night. Notably, the vigilant presence of ART the Dalmatian, a towering 19.5-foot fiberglass sculpture guarding the former fire station turned Central ARTSTATION, comes alive after sunset with dynamic LED spots, treating visitors to a mesmerizing symphony of color.

801 Crockett St., Shreveport, 318-673-6537
shreveportcommon.com

TIP

Download the Shreveport Common app for a map of the historical places, attractions, and public art in the area.

CONNECT TO ART
AT A LOCAL MUSEUM

SBC visitors can enjoy a variety of art galleries. The Southern University Museum of Art celebrates African American art. The Bossier Arts Council's artist galleries host rotating exhibits featuring art forms from paintings to photography, including a Clyde Connell.

The Bailey Gallery stands as a testament to the power of contemporary art. The Andress Artist & Entrepreneur Center is dedicated to nurturing local talent and serves as an artist launchpad. Artspace is an experimental space that fosters creativity and community engagement.

The Marlene Yu Museum is a world of abstract art displaying the energetic creations of Marlene Yu. R. W. Norton Art Gallery has an extensive collection of art and artifacts from various periods and cultures. They are best known for their Remington pieces and stunning gardens. Meadows Museum of Art features an impressive collection of world cultures and traditions.

TIP

If you visit the Bossier Arts Council's artist galleries, ask to take a trip upstairs to see their hidden Mural Stairwell where artwork by Bossier students cover the walls and stairwell. Afterward, grab a $5 token, visit their Art-o-Mat machine, and walk away with a mini piece of artwork from the only Art-o-Mat in North Louisiana!

OTHER SHREVEPORT MUSEUMS AND GALLERIES

Southern University Museum of Art
610 Texas St., Ste. 110, Shreveport, 318-670-9631
susla.edu/page/university-museum

Bossier Arts Council's Artist Galleries
630 Barksdale Blvd., Bossier City, 318-741-8310
bossierarts.org

Bailey Gallery
214 Texas St., Shreveport, 318-424-6764
bailey-gallery.com

Andress Artist & Entrepreneur Center
717 Crockett St., Shreveport, 318-218-1845
aaec.space

artspace
708 Texas St., Shreveport, 318-673-6535
artspaceshreveport.com

Meadows Museum of Art
2911 Centenary Blvd., Shreveport, 318-869-5169
themeadowsmuseum.com

Marlene Yu Museum
710 Travis St., Shreveport, 318-717-9111
marleneyumuseum.org

R. W. Norton Art Gallery
4747 Creswell Ave., Shreveport, 318-865-4201
rwnaf.org

LEARN THE POWER OF THE MIGHTY RED
AT THE J. BENNETT JOHNSTON
WATERWAY REGIONAL VISITOR CENTER

At the J. Bennett Johnston Waterway Regional Visitor Center, guests of all ages are invited to learn about the history of the Red River, spanning both its past and present.

This center serves as a testament to the dedicated efforts of the Corps of Engineers, who harnessed the power of the mighty Red for both navigation and recreation. The 8,300 square feet facility features a welcoming reception area, a theater, and an impressive exhibition hall with audiovisual, static, and interactive exhibits. The multipurpose theater treats guests to a continuous film about the alluring Red River.

As a regional visitor center, it proudly represents the states through which the Red River flows, including New Mexico, Texas, Oklahoma, Arkansas, and Louisiana.

700 Clyde Fant Pkwy., Shreveport, 318-677-2673
mvk.usace.army.mil/missions/recreation/j-bennett-johnston-visitor-center

---

TIP

On-site, the public can access complimentary travel brochures and recreational pamphlets for Louisiana, Arkansas, Texas, Oklahoma, and New Mexico.

CREATE
A CUSTOM GLASS PIECE
AT A GLASSBLOWING STUDIO

Be entranced by the world of glass art at Sanctuary Glass Studio or High Gravity Glassworks in Shreveport. These esteemed studios offer an exceptional experience for art connoisseurs and aspiring glass artists alike.

Delight in the mesmerizing displays of intricate glasswork, from delicate sculptures to gleaming glassware. Watch a demonstration and learn about the history, process, and equipment used. Consider commissioning a custom piece, tailored to your preferences and vision, as a unique memento or a thoughtful gift. Alternatively, unleash your creativity by participating in hands-on workshops where skilled artisans will guide you through the process of creating your very own glass masterpiece!

Embrace the magic of glass and take home a one-of-a-kind treasure to forever cherish your time in Shreveport.

Sanctuary Glass Studio
423 Lake St., Shreveport, 504-390-4377
sanctuaryartsschool.org

High Gravity Glassworks
1200 Marshall St., Ste. 500, Shreveport, 318-582-1424
highgravityglassworks.com

JOURNEY THROUGH TIME
AT THE BOSSIER PARISH
LIBRARY HISTORY CENTER

The Bossier Parish Library History Center is a portal to the past steeped in its rich heritage. This center offers a treasure trove of historical insights and exhibits.

Delve into the annals of time through an assortative collection of artifacts, documents, photographs, and interactive displays that vividly narrate the region's compelling story. From Native American roots to the modern era, the history center chronicles the evolution of Bossier Parish, highlighting its cultural, social, and economic transformations.

Be enlightened by educational programs, guided tours, and expert lectures that celebrate the local legacy and foster a deeper understanding of the area's heritage. In addition to historical resources and programs, the library also offers coffee chats and DIY craft programs.

2206 Beckett St., Bossier City, 318-746-7717
live-bossierlibrary-v3.pantheonsite.io/locations/history-center

VOYAGE THROUGH THE HISTORY OF AIRPOWER
AT BARKSDALE AIR FORCE BASE

The Barksdale Global Power Museum on Barksdale Air Force Base in Bossier City is a tribute to aviation and military heritage.

This museum boasts an impressive array of impeccably preserved aircraft, artifacts, and exhibits that illuminate the valorous journeys of aviators and their pivotal missions.

Get an up-close look at iconic aircraft, including the esteemed B-17 and B-24 bombers of World War II, accompanied by their stalwart companion, the P-51 Mustang. Discover Cold War legends like the B-52D and B-52G Stratofortress, as well as the unparalleled MACH 3-plus SR-71 Blackbird. Inside, you will find six exhibits that vividly narrate the base's storied past, including a World War II–era briefing room featuring a compelling 20-minute video.

Come and pay tribute to the US Air Force and the massive technology used to safeguard our skies.

88 Shreveport Rd., Bossier City, 318-456-2840
barksdaleglobalpowermuseum.com

TIP
Clearance to this museum must be made through email 30 days in advance. Go to their website to obtain the proper form and email address.

MARDI ON
AT THE KREWE OF GEMINI MARDI GRAS MUSEUM

What happens on the float stays on the float (and in the Krewe of Gemini Mardi Gras Museum). Absorb the history of the iconic Mardi Gras celebration through a splendid collection of dazzling costumes, intricate floats, and carnival artifacts.

The 10,000 square feet museum is an ever-evolving treasure, continually updating and expanding its displays. Considered a work in progress, this museum collection represents over a decade of Mardi Gras fun in North Louisiana. As a versatile venue, the museum is not only a cultural hub but also a sought-after location for special events. Its doors only open from January through March with limited days and hours.

Be sure to catch this magical celebration of the Mardi Gras spirit while you can.

2101 E Texas St., Bossier City, 318-741-9264
kreweofgemini.com

OBSERVE A 1,000-YEAR-OLD LOG BOAT
AT THE LOUISIANA STATE EXHIBIT MUSEUM

Learn about Louisiana's architectural and artistic heritage at the Louisiana State Exhibit Museum, a masterpiece born from the New Deal's public works initiatives in 1939.

This circular marvel, an embodiment of ultramodern style, gleams with opulent marble, granite, and polished aluminum, enveloping a landscaped courtyard adorned with hand-cut limestone. A testament to the era's grandeur, the museum possesses an astonishing fresco by muralist Conrad Albrizio and meticulously crafted dioramas, capturing a vivid snapshot of 1930s Louisiana life. Within the rotunda, arresting murals by local artists graphically depict the state's landscapes and history.

The West Wing gallery hosts fascinating rotating art exhibits, while the museum's treasure trove includes extensive Native American artifacts, highlighted by the remarkable 1,000-year-old, 30-foot Caddo culture log boat.

3015 Greenwood Rd., Shreveport, 318-632-2020
laexhibitmuseum.org

PAINT, LAUGH, AND SIP
AT ARTIPSY

Artipsy, where the celebration never stops and creativity thrives! What better way to keep the good times rolling than by painting the town with your favorite people, jamming to live grooves, and joining in on special Artipsy programs.

Sip on signature cocktails like frozen margarita buckets that truly set the mood. From ladies' nights to comedy shows, bingo, woodcrafts, dinners, and music, Artipsy offers an eclectic range of entertainment. And who could forget those illustrious date nights? At Artipsy, the canvas is your playground, and the party never stops as you let your imagination and spirits run wild.

When it is time for all the fun of the evening to end, you get to leave with your very own original piece of artwork to commemorate the night.

450 Clyde Fant Pkwy., Ste. 600, Shreveport, 318-670-8217
artipsystudio.com

DISCOVER WATER PURIFICATION HISTORY
AT THE SHREVEPORT WATER WORKS MUSEUM

The Shreveport Water Works and Railroad Museum is an extraordinary site where history and engineering converge.

The McNeill Street Pumping Station, a National Historic Landmark and National Historic Civil Engineering Landmark, houses the museum. Established in 1887, it pioneered advanced filtration techniques, including early adoption of chlorine treatment in 1911.

Notably, it held the distinction of being the last operational steam-powered municipal water works in the United States until 1980. Explore this remarkable preserved facility on guided or self-guided tours, observing antique steam equipment and learning about water purification through time. Partnering with the Shreveport Railroad Museum, the site also displays historic North Louisiana railroad artifacts, revealing steam's role in transportation.

The railroad exhibits are in the auxiliary building and include a captivating HO-scale model railroad depicting 1960s downtown Shreveport.

142 N Common St., Shreveport, 318-221-3388
shreveportwaterworks.org

TOUR RESTORED PLANTATION STRUCTURES
AT THE LSUS PIONEER HERITAGE CENTER

Step back in time as you tour seven meticulously restored plantation structures, each revealing unique facets of pioneer life. Among them, the iconic Thrasher House and Caspiana House, both listed on the National Register of Historic Places, offer a glimpse into antebellum architecture and lifestyles.

The Webb & Webb Commissary is a turn-of-the-century plantation store, while the Blacksmith Shop showcases working equipment and craftsmanship. The Detached Kitchen reveals pioneer culinary practices, and the Doctor's Office transports you to early medical practices. The Riverfront Mission adds depth to the narrative, with interesting stories of its many purposes since 1930.

Commendable educational programs and community outreach make the LSUS Pioneer Heritage Center stand out as a testament to preservation, providing an authentic journey through Louisiana history.

One University Pl., Shreveport, 318-797-5339
lsus.edu/community/pioneer-heritage-center

TIP
Tours are by appointment only. To schedule a visit, call or email pioneer@lsus.edu.

TRAVEL IN TIME TO 1800S SHREVEPORT
AT THE SPRING STREET MUSEUM

From Native American heritage to the monumental feat of Captain Henry Miller Shreve clearing the Great Raft Log Jam and beyond, get to know the evolution of the area.

Housed within one of Shreveport's oldest buildings, this museum beautifully preserves its history dating back to the Civil War era. The Spring Street Museum, a National Historic Landmark since 1979, still maintains its original interior and exterior. Guests can expect a journey through time, with vintage clothing, antique toys, firearms, photographs, and more.

Traverse the halls where banks and businesses once thrived, and explore the meticulously restored Victorian parlor, transporting you to the late 1800s. Step into the essence of Shreveport's past at the Spring Street Museum, where every artifact unveils a piece of the city's compelling story.

525 Spring St., Shreveport, 318-562-3128
springstreetmuseum.org

ANOTHER MUSEUM OF SPECIALIZED LOCAL HISTORY
Talbot Medical Museum
2105 Airline Dr., Bossier City, 318-212-8472

MARVEL AT ORNATE ARCHITECTURE
AT HISTORICAL SHREVEPORT LANDMARKS

Go on a mission to find the many historical buildings and landmarks in the area. The Antioch Baptist Church stands as a cornerstone of African American history, representing resilience and faith. The Ogilvie-Wiener Mansion is over 100 years old and was featured in the opening credits of HBO's *True Blood*.

The Caddo Parish Courthouse is an architectural masterpiece that has been the nucleus of legal proceedings for generations. Holy Trinity Catholic Church, with its intricate Romanesque design stands as the oldest church in Shreveport. Oakland Cenetery harbors stories of the region's pioineers and the graves of about 800 yellow fever victims. The Elvis Presley and James Burton statues pay homage to the artists' impact on music. The Huddie "Lead Belly" Ledbetter statue honors an icon who gave voice to the spirit of the South.

TIP

Call Trudeau History Tours at 318-272-6045 to schedule a guided historical walking tour of downtown Shreveport. Email history professor Dr. Cheryl White at Cheryl.white@lsus.edu to schedule a group tour of the Oakland Cemetery.

SEVERAL HISTORICAL LANDMARKS IN SHREVEPORT

Antioch Baptist Church
1057 Texas Ave.

Ogilvie-Wiener Mansion
728 Austen Pl.

Caddo Parish Courthouse
501 Texas St., Ste. 103

Holy Trinity Catholic Church
315 Marshall St.

Oakland Cemetery
1000 Milam St.

James Burton and Elvis Presley Statues
Municipal Auditorium
714 Elvis Presley Ave.

Huddie "Lead Belly" Ledbetter Statue
416 Texas St.

Logan Mansion
725 Austen Pl.

Church of the Holy Cross
875 Cotton St.

B'Nai Zion Temple
802 Cotton St.

Calanthean Temple
1007 ½ Texas St.

Scottish Rite Cathedral
725 Cotton St.

STAY AT
A FAIRFIELD AVENUE
HISTORIC BED & BREAKFAST

While visiting Shreveport-Bossier, you will need a place to rest your head. For an experience beyond the average hotel chain, book a room at one of the bed & breakfast homes on the historic Fairfield Ave. Each offers a unique blend of hospitality and historic allure dating back as early as 1870. Experience the elegance of carefully restored Victorian mansions with modern amenities. They indulge their guests in Southern hospitality with cozy rooms and personalized service to create a home away from home feeling. The esthetics exude timeless charm, blending antiques with contemporary comforts such as hot tubs and wifi. Waking to a hardy breakfast that consists of homemade muffins, cereals, fresh fruit, eggs, sausage, and more will fuel you for a day of touring Shreveport-Bossier.

2349 Fairfield "A Bed & Breakfast"
2439 Fairfield Ave., Shreveport, 318-424-2424
shreveportbedandbreakfast.com

Fairfield Place
2221 Fairfield Ave., Shreveport, 318-848-7776
stayfairfield.com

Fairfield Manor
2300 Fairfield Ave., Shreveport, 318-848-7776
stayfairfield.com

Bella Nonnas Olive Oil & Vinegar Tasting Bar

SHOPPING
AND FASHION

PERFECT YOUR LOOK
AT THE PAPER TULIP

The Paper Tulip has become Shreveport's go-to destination for invitations, stationery, and gifts. Enjoy a personalized shopping experience as you explore the latest trends in paper, printing processes, and design.

Additionally, they have a chic boutique with an exquisite selection of designer clothing by renowned brands like Lilly Pulitzer. Complete your outfit with exceptional extras, including bags, accessories, purses, and jewelry. Looking for a unique gift? The Paper Tulip has you covered there too with a variety of one-of-a-kind treasures. Add a personalized touch with monogramming services available for cups, wineglasses, and bags.

Whether you are hunting for the perfect ensemble for any season or seeking that jaw-dropping look for a special occasion, their friendly fashion consultants will be happy to assist you.

5823 Youree Dr., Shreveport, 318-869-3123
thepapertulipshreveport.com

TASTE THE WORLD'S FINEST OLIVE OILS AND VINEGARS
AT BELLA NONNAS

Give way to the world of exquisite flavors at Bella Nonnas Olive Oil & Vinegar Tasting Bar. They meticulously source their oils from both the Northern and Southern Hemispheres, ensuring the freshest and healthiest options available.

Their balsamic vinegars hail from Modena, Italy, free from any additional sweeteners, artificial coloring, or flavoring. With an impressive array of infused oils and vinegars like blood orange, garlic, and Tuscan herb, Bella Nonnas invites you to sniff, swirl, and sip your way through a sensory experience like no other. Sample the grassy freshness of single cultivar oils and savor the richness of infused varieties that will elevate your culinary creations to new heights.

At Bella Nonnas, you will unlock a world of taste and refinement that goes beyond the ordinary grocery store selection.

1409 E 70th St., Ste. 107, Shreveport, 318-798-6602
bellanonnasoils.com

BUY FRESH
AT LOCAL FARMERS MARKETS

Jellied, jarred, and fresh fruits and veggies, and freshly baked bread, are a part of the agricultural offerings of Shreveport-Bossier's farms and farmers markets.

The Shreveport Farmers' Market (June through August) at Festival Plaza and the Bossier City Farmers Market and Night Market (April through November) at the Pierre Bossier Mall parking lot are two of the most popular destinations to shop.

For a unique agricultural twist, visit Cotton St. Farms, where you will see firsthand the unconventional method of soilless produce growth. For a hands-on experience, head to Ryan Farms Produce, offering you-pick opportunities for fresh greens, tomatoes, sweet potatoes, and more. During the fall season, head over to the enchanting Dixie Maze Farms, where you can frolic in pumpkin patches, corn mazes, haunted trails, murder mystery dinners, and a myriad of other attractions that celebrate the essence of agriculture in Shreveport-Bossier.

TIP

Do not miss the prepared-from-scratch and made-to-order dishes at the Shreveport Farmers' Market. They are some of the best in the area. Also, some of the merchants listed above only take cash, so come prepared.

OTHER PLACES TO BUY LOCAL PRODUCE

Bossier City Farmers Market and Night Market
2950 E Texas St., Bossier City
bossiercityfarmersmarket.com
bossiernightmarket.com/home.html

Shreveport Farmers' Market
101 Crockett St., Shreveport
redriverrevel.com/farmers-market

Cotton St. Farms
406 Cotton St., Shreveport, 225-963-0956
cottonstfarms.com

Ryan Farms Produce
8172 Dixie-Shreveport Rd., Shreveport, 318-425-3004
ryanfarmsproduce.com

Dixie Maze Farms
9596 Sentell Rd., Shreveport, 318-703-2870
dixiemaze.com

GET PERSONALIZED GIFTS
AT LEWIS'

Lewis' gift shop, a staple in Shreveport's retail scene for over 75 years, is a testament to the Lewis family's dedication to providing exceptional service.

From its humble beginnings as a neighborhood drugstore with a soda fountain, gifts, and sundries, Lewis' has evolved into a stunning showcase. The drugstore may no longer exist, but the gift shop spans an impressive 10,000 square feet; the showroom exudes an old-world charm while offering a contemporary and stylish shopping experience.

The Lewis family takes pride in their long-standing relationship with valued customers, ensuring that everyone receives the utmost attention and care. Encounter the allure of Lewis' and explore their extensive range of products including personalized monogramming and engraving.

5807 Youree Dr., Shreveport, 318-868-6700
lewisgifts.com

FIND
YOUR PERFECT SCENT
AT CLEAN SLATE BOTANICALS

Located in the Andress Artist and Entrepreneur Center, Clean Slate Botanicals beckons with its mission to intertwine nature and well-being.

Discover a symphony of scents designed to harmonize with your home and skin while upholding eco-safety and skin-friendly standards. From candles that illuminate your space to linen sprays that transform it, and from enriching face and skin care to nourishing body oils and butters, Clean Slate Botanicals offers a range of products that elevate both mood and atmosphere.

Take off on a sensory journey, where each product resonates with nature's essence. Additionally, embrace the chance to craft your own memories through their candle pouring experiences. This unique opportunity not only fosters connection and creativity among friends but leaves you with a one-of-a-kind candle, encapsulating the spirit of Clean Slate Botanicals.

4832 Line Ave., Shreveport, 312-806-7977
cleanslatebotanicals.com

DRESS IN A WORK OF ART
AT ABSOLUTELY ABIGAIL'S

Absolutely Abigail's is a charming boutique located in Shreveport. This shop offers a true boutique shopping experience like no other.

From the moment you stride through the doors, you'll be captivated by its warm and inviting atmosphere. Absolutely Abigail's displays a carefully curated selection of clothing, jewelry, scarves, socks, and handbags, all handpicked with impeccable taste.

If you are searching for an outfit that could also be considered a work of art, this boutique will be the paint to your canvas. Let the friendly and knowledgeable staff dress you from head to toe in their unique pieces, ensuring a personalized shopping experience. With its blend of retro classics, trendy pieces, and art-driven apparel, Absolutely Abigail's caters to a wide range of styles and preferences.

3795 Youree Dr., Shreveport, 318-219-0788
absolutely-abigails.myshopify.com

MORE FABULOUS BOUTIQUES

Favorite Sisters' Boutique
5723 Youree Dr., Shreveport, 318-861-0580
favsistersboutique.com

Lena's Shoe Gallery
501 Milam St., Shreveport, 318-424-0272
lenasshoegallery.com

Jaded the Boutique
1605 Benton Rd., Ste. J, Bossier City, 318-752-5663
jadedtheboutique.shop

K Couture Boutique Bossier
2850 Douglas Dr., Ste. H, Bossier City, 318-746-1414
shopkcouture.com

Krush Boutique
4801 Line Ave., Ste. 2, Shreveport, 318-865-4773
facebook.com/krushtherunway

La Bambolina
6505 Line Ave., Ste. 20, Shreveport, 318-861-1616
facebook.com/labambolinaboutique

LBD by Design
1370 E 70th St., Ste. 700, Shreveport, 318-562-3300
lbdbydesign.com

M. Clothes/Shoes/Lifestyle
855 Pierremont Rd., Ste. 128, Shreveport, 318-220-8828
mshreveport.com

BRING HOME
SOME SOUTHERN CHARM
AT BIRDWELL'S

Birdwell's is a gifting and home furnishing store in Bossier City that draws inspiration from southern tradition, style, and nostalgia.

Their "Happy Hour" collection offers spirits-themed decor and glasses for elevating your cocktail experience. The "Front Porch" collection transports you to nostalgic days of front porch gatherings and sipping refreshing lemonade. Find solace and inspiration in the "Gotta Have Faith" collection, featuring faith symbols that add grace to your surroundings. Experience the hospitality and charm of the "Home and Gifting" section, carefully curated to represent the southern lifestyle. The "Tailgating Time" collection is filled with game-day gear for the ultimate football experience. The "Tucked In" collection displays pretty things and heartfelt sentiments. Lastly, find the perfect souvenirs to take home to a friend in their under $50 area.

2151 Airline Dr., Ste. 1100, Bossier City, 318-584-7299
shopbirdwells.com

PURCHASE CUSTOMIZED SOUVENIRS
AT APPLI-KS

Appli-Ks Embroidery & Gifts is an excellent shop for personalized treasures in Shreveport. They have a true legacy of excellence and a string of accolades, including the esteemed title of "Best Monogram Store in Shreveport Bossier" for both 2021 and 2022, as recognized by *SB Magazine*.

As soon as you walk in the door, you will quickly discover the exceptional craftsmanship and attention to detail that sets this boutique apart.

Offering an impressive range of custom embroidery services, Appli-Ks transforms everyday items into unique keepsakes. Whether it is monogrammed linens, personalized apparel, or custom gifts, their skilled team and cutting-edge technology brings your vision to life with impeccable precision. Beyond embroidery, Appli-Ks also curates a large collection of charming gifts, clothing, and accessories that cater to every occasion.

616 Texas St., Shreveport, 318-562-3713
appli-ks.com

PICK UP
SOUVENIRS WITH A SIDE
OF POWER TOOLS
AT TUBBS HARDWARE

Tubbs Hardware is an adored institution in Bossier City that carries tools, power equipment, hunting blinds, deer feeders, grills, lawn equipment, and outdoor furniture.

As you step into this iconic store, you'll be greeted by rows upon rows of tools, supplies, and equipment, making it a go-to destination for both professional contractors and DIYers. Building upon its rich history, Tubbs Hardware has also made a name for itself as the Louisiana souvenir and Mardi Gras headquarters.

They carry a wide range of Cajun-themed gifts and food that celebrates the unique culture and flavors of Louisiana. And do not miss their culinary masterpiece, Tubbs X-Treme King Cake! This delectable dish is a must-try for anyone seeking the authentic taste of Mardi Gras.

615 Benton Rd., Bossier City, 318-746-0311
tubbshardware.com

STOCK UP ON LSU MERCHANDISE
AT THE VACUUM CLEANER HOSPITAL

Like Tubbs Hardware, the Vacuum Cleaner Hospital is a place where you enter expecting one thing and you get so much more.

As the name suggests, this shop specializes in all things related to vacuum cleaners, offering a wide selection of cleaners and supplies to keep your home spick and span. However, that is not all you will find here.

Prepare to be delighted by a treasure trove of gift items, candles, home decor, and garden accessories. Sports enthusiasts will be thrilled to explore the collection of college football memorabilia, including LSU Tigers–themed merchandise. Fleur-de-lis accessories add a touch of local flair, while hand soaps and bags make for practical yet stylish finds.

The Vacuum Cleaner Hospital is another great place to find a unique gift or treat yourself to something special while visiting Shreveport.

8959 Jewella Ave., Shreveport, 318-688-1331
facebook.com/vacuumcleanerhospital

INVEST IN LOUISIANA-THEMED DINNERWARE
AT JOLIE BLONDE GIFTS

Jolie Blonde Gifts is a classy shopping experience located in southeast Shreveport. This charming boutique sells highly unique pieces including LSU gear for the most fashionable of fans.

Explore their collection of trendy accessories, jewelry, scarves, and handbags. Take pleasure in their whimsical home decor items such as decorative pillows and wall art. Discover a variety of Louisiana-themed gifts that add an extra touch of thoughtfulness.

Whether you are seeking a thank-you gift, a special occasion memento, game day essentials, stylish home decor, kitchenware, bath products, or a spontaneous surprise for a loved one, Jolie Blonde Gifts has a curated selection that caters to your needs. To make your shopping experience even more convenient, they offer free gift wrapping and local delivery within Shreveport.

9210 Wallace Lake Rd., Ste. A, Shreveport, 318-773-1055
jolieblondegiftsla.com

MORE GIFT SHOPS

Giftspace at Artspace
708 Texas St., Shreveport, 318-673-6535
artspaceshreveport.com

The Enchanted Garden
2429 Line Ave., Shreveport, 318-227-1213
facebook.com/enchantedgardenshreveport

False River Gift Shop
1700 Old Minden Rd., Ste. 141, Bossier City, 318-747-6660
ralphandkacoos.com

The Peace of Mind Center
3611 Youree Dr., Shreveport, 318-219-8344
thepeaceofmindcenter.com

UNCOVER RARE TREASURE
AT AMERICAN COINS & COLLECTIBLES

American Coins & Collectibles is a haven for numismatists and collectors alike. This esteemed establishment specializes in rare coins, currency, and an extensive range of collectibles.

This place will ignite your passion for history and treasures with its display of coins from different eras, including US and international pieces. Beyond coins, American Coins & Collectibles also carries a remarkable assortment of other items, including sports memorabilia, vintage toys, and unique artifacts. The knowledgeable staff are always on hand to assist you in finding that special piece to enhance your collection or to help you embark on a new collecting journey.

Add American Coins & Collectibles to your shopping itinerary for a special experience filled with history, intrigue, and the thrill of finding rare and valuable treasures.

855 Pierremont Rd., Ste. 123, Shreveport, 800-865-3562
amercoins.wpcomstaging.com

MORE PLACES TO GO ANTIQUING

Antiques on Gladstone
755 Gladstone Blvd., Shreveport, 318-868-2940
antiquesongladstone.com

Timeline Antiques and Collectibles Mall
3323 Line Ave., Shreveport, 318-861-0808
facebook.com/timelineantiquesandcollectiblesmall

Kitty's Kitsch
3311 Line Ave., Shreveport, 318-621-7508
kittys-kitsch.business.site

Antique Shoppes at 1100 Barksdale
1100 Barksdale Blvd., Bossier City, 318-658-9766
antiqueshoppesat1100barksdale.com

C&C Mercantile & Lighting
1110 Texas Ave., Shreveport, 318-632-1028
facebook.com/ccmercantileshreveport

SHOP UNTIL YOU DROP
AT THE LOUISIANA
BOARDWALK OUTLETS

The Louisiana Boardwalk Outlets is situated along the scenic riverfront between East Texas Street and I-20 and hosts many attractions for people of all ages. Start your adventure at the renowned Bass Pro Shops, where the outdoorsy types can find everything they need for their next adventure. Enjoy a movie at the modern theater or try your luck in the arcade.

With a variety of restaurants to choose from, you can dine while taking in picturesque views of the river. Shop until you drop at outlet stores like Levi's, Kay Jewelers, and Express, and excite the kids with trolley and carousel rides.

For those looking to extend their stay, the Margaritaville Resort Casino on the north end of the property offers luxurious accommodations and entertainment.

540 Boardwalk Blvd., Bossier City, 318-752-1455
louisianaboardwalk.com

A MORE TRADITIONAL OUTDOOR SHOPPING MALL
Shoppes at Bellemead
6535 Youree Dr., Shreveport, 318-222-2244
shoppesatbellemead.com

LISTEN TO VINTAGE RECORDS ON HIGH-QUALITY STEREO SYSTEMS
AT THE LITTLE SHOP OF MUSIC

Brimming with a curated selection of stereo equipment, guitars, music-related artwork, and records, this shop is more than just a store; it is a celebration of Louisiana's musical history! Hang out in a guitar room adorned with vintage and used guitars, alongside amplifiers, inviting you to try and play to your heart's content. Browse shelves lined with rare vinyl, CDs, local music, guitar equipment, vintage stereo gear, music books, and music-related artwork. The Little Shop of Music is more than a store—it is a communal hub where music lovers gather.

1055 Louisiana Ave., Shreveport, 318-518-9672
thelittleshopofmusic.com

ANOTHER ROCKING MUSIC STORE
Rick's Records
3512 Youree Dr., Shreveport, 318-868-4268
withthefamilyentertainment.com

BLEND
COMFORT AND STYLE
AT NADER'S GALLERY

This sibling partnership has cultivated one of the most exceptional and motivating environments to date. The gallery area has undergone an expansion, growing from 1,000 square feet to an expansive 10,000 square feet, granting ample room to accommodate the region's largest and most unparalleled collection of contemporary art and furniture.

Nader's Gallery has been recognized by the *318 Forum Magazine* as one of the city's top five most intriguing spaces. Here, you will discover products that are both visually captivating and of remarkable quality, unattainable anywhere else. The selection, thoughtfully curated from sources as far-reaching as New York, Italy, London, Paris, and beyond, reflects affordability without compromise.

They have fostered a lively and laid-back ambiance to facilitate your quest for pieces that seamlessly blend comfort with style.

524 E Kings Hwy., Shreveport, 318-868-3021
nadersgallery.com

TIP
They are only open Tuesday through Thursday from 9:30 a.m. to 5:30 p.m.

OTHER SHOPS THAT FEATURE LOCAL ARTISTS' WORK

318 Art Co.
750 Southfield Rd., Ste. A, Shreveport, 318-626-5439
318artco.com

The Agora Borealis
421 Lake St., Shreveport, 318-268-3011
theagoraborealis.com

ACTIVITIES
BY SEASON

SPRING

Make Sand Art at ArtBreak, 95

Get Spicy at Crawdaddy's Kitchen, 3

Pinch a Tail at Shane's Seafood & BarBQ, 30

Visit the Largest Park Dedicated to Roses at the American Rose Center, 40

Bike or Fish at the Red River, 80

Explore Ecosystems and Wildlife at the Red River National Wildlife Refuge, 85

Embark on a Public Art Works Scavenger Hunt at Shreveport Common, 96

SUMMER

Honor Our Great Nation at Freedom Fest, 53

Cool Off with a Sweet Treat, 28

Float the Lazy River at Splash Kingdom Oasis, 77

Picnic at a Local Park, 82

Buy Fresh at Local Farmers Markets, 118

FALL

WINTER

SUGGESTED
ITINERARIES

DATE NIGHT

Shuck Some Oysters at the Oyster Bar and Grille, 11

Spike Your Coffee at Another Broken Egg Cafe, 21

Appreciate a Grand Pianist Fine-Dining Atmosphere at 2 Johns, 22

Place a Bet at a Riverboat Casino, 38

Test Your Wits at Escape SBC, 67

Witness the Magic of the Bakowski Bridge of Lights at Glo Fest, 41

Grab a Bite to Eat While Touring Downtown Shreveport, 8

Shop Until You Drop at the Louisiana Boardwalk Outlets, 132

Visit the Largest Park Dedicated to Roses at the American Rose Center, 40

Play like a Pro at Surge Entertainment, 89

FAMILY FUN

Zip-Line over Alligators at Gators & Friends, 74

Cool Off with a Sweet Treat, 28

Start Your Engine at Party Central Family Fun Center, 65

Float the Lazy River at Splash Kingdom Oasis, 77

Knock Down Some Pins at Holiday Lanes, 64

Fly through the Galaxy at Sci-Port Discovery Center, 70

Bounce to New Heights at a Trampoline Park, 76

Spot Chimpanzees in Their Forest Habitats, 73

LIVE MUSIC AND LIBATIONS

LOUISIANA CULTURE

• •

ARTISTIC VIBE

SPORTY SPOTS

HISTORY TRIP

FOODIE FAVORITES

• •

FREE AND FUN

INDEX